AN UNEXAMINED LIFE

D1522057

Robert N. Chan

Dedication

To my son Adam who won't make the same mistakes I have but will make more intelligent ones.

We are here on Earth to fart around, and don't let anybody tell you any different.

—Kurt Vonnegut

If you're going to tell people the truth, be funny or they'll kill you.

—Billy Wilder

CONTENTS

INTRODUCTION

At his trial for impiety and corrupting youth, Socrates, the wisest man in ancient Greece, famously said, "An unexamined life is not worth living." No wonder the court sentenced him to death by hemlock.

As you'll see, my life, although unexamined, has clearly been worth living; and I trust you'll find much of it amusing. I've made all my significant decisions with the same insouciance I devoted to determining whether to have fries or salad with my double cheeseburger. Bad example since fries were always the obvious choice. No need to care about cholesterol if you don't have it checked.[1]

Not that my major life decisions have worked out so great, but I doubt that they'd have turned out better if I'd given them careful consideration. All such choices turn on assumptions about the future, and as the world-renowned pundit Yogi Berra is reputed to have said, "The hardest thing to predict is the future." Since life is a roll of the dice, the thing to do is go with your gut. Approximately a hundred trillion bacteria inhabit your gut; given those numbers, they must be onto something.

According to the Buddha, life consists of suffering, pain, and misery caused by selfish craving and personal desire. With all due respect to the Awakened One, my experience has been precisely the opposite. Like a shark who must keep moving or perish, I've thrived on conflict. Most of my suffering, pain, and misery has resulted from

---

[1] LEGAL NOTICE: While this autobiography is replete with many such pearls of wisdom, I take no responsibility for any negative consequences that may result from following the advice contained herein. I employ the word *herein* to give the sentence an ineffable legal heft.

the three horsemen of my personal apocalypse: inactivity, boredom, and ennui. Striving to satisfy goals and desires has led to happiness.

So who are you going to believe—Socrates; the Lord Buddha, Siddhartha Gautama; or me? Sure, I'm an underdog in this battle for your hearts and minds. But keep an open mind, and for the love of God, ignore the promptings of your hearts.

I retired just as COVID hit. The loneliness and dislocation that accompanied the lockdown took a heavy emotional toll. Never one to pass up the opportunity for foolish futility in the face of adversity, I deluded myself into believing that there was a readership for the humorous autobiography of a baby boomer who came of age during the countercultural upheavals of the '60s and early '70s and practiced law in New York City—the commercial capital of the world and epicenter of all that's good and holy—and then struggled with the travails of retirement, the plague, debilitating injuries, and aging. That may not sound like fertile ground for humor but read on. You'll be amused by my efforts if only via schadenfreude over my failures. Also, as I'm emotionally fragile, your rejection could have a deleterious effect on my health and well-being. Surely, you don't want that on your conscience.

The irony isn't lost on me that writing about an unexamined life requires the self-examination that I've dedicated my life to avoiding. Irony is one of my few areas of expertise. To rationalize this dramatic departure from past practice, I told myself that self-examination would, via a kind of alchemy, transform the base metal of my disparate recollections into coherent literary gold. I'm too caught up in self-delusion to determine to what degree, if any, this has happened. But I promise this autobiography will be a laugh a minute—if you're a highly skilled speed reader. Otherwise, maybe a laugh every other hour or so.

As an incentive for you to read on, I, for a limited time only, offer an unprecedented guaranty. If, after reading this book, you ultimately fail to obtain everlasting life, admission to heaven's most exclusive country club, *and* forty virgins of your preferred gender and erotic predilection(s), I'll refund twice the purchase price, less postage, and handling.

My take on the world might strike you as odd but understand that it's unimaginably weird to be seventy-fucking-five, which is the oldest I've ever been. Every old person is an immigrant in his own land, but I tell myself age has given me perspective and even wisdom. If that illusion can work for Joe Biden, it should work for me. Hmm, as I write this, it doesn't seem to be working so well for Scranton Joe. He, however, has five big years on me; and one man's wisdom and perspective is another's folly and delusion.

I

I Owe Everything I Am Today to My Father

1948–1962

I owe everything I am today to my father, but I'm not resentful—well, only a little.

It could be argued, but not by me, that I have no one to blame but myself. Also, as I'm only seventy-five, my life could still turn around.

I never felt that my father loved me or took anything I did seriously, at least until I entered the working world. I'm hardly alone in that. The fanatical need to gain approval from emotionally detached fathers—even long after those dads had passed on—has driven many of us emotionally deprived boys to monomaniacally pursue greatness, obscurity, or self-destructive failure or, in my case, a peculiar combination of the three.

Winston Churchill's parents, for example, shipped him off to boarding school when he turned seven, as was the practice among the English upper class in those days. Unusual even by the standards of the time, his father ignored him. Occupied with his efforts to climb the greasy political pole and suffering from tertiary syphilis, Lord Randolph mostly didn't respond to Winston's long pleading letters. But when he did, his responses combined coldness with withering disapproval. Winston never ate a meal with his parents until he was in his teens, and even then, he ate with them only on rare occasions. As a typically perverse result, Winston admired his dad above all others and spent his life seeking the approval he never got. Not that I'm drawing an equivalence. I neither smoked cigars nor wore a jumpsuit in the Blitz. Like Britain's wartime prime minister, though, and like many of us insufficiently loved sons, I worshipped my father—not that he seemed to notice or care either.

I've long felt that there's an emptiness inside me that can't be satisfied, an unquenchable, unrequited thirst for love paired with a drive to sabotage those efforts, as set forth in painful detail in the following chapters. None of that makes me unusual. But at least, unlike some, I recognize the problem. Luckily, the problem is so fucking obvious that realizing it required barely a scintilla of self-examination. As to the solution . . . perhaps reincarnation.

Would I have turned out differently—better, happier, more loving, more successful, more in touch with my feelings—if I'd had more emotive and loving parents? No way to know. Will writing this autobiography help me to understand my feelings and better deal with them? Isn't it pretty to think so?

When I was ten or so, I asked my dad why he never came to watch my Little League games. He responded, "Do you watch me play golf?" End of discussion.

I was a married successful lawyer and my sister, Janet, was a married respected magazine editor. Unbeknownst to us, she was trying to get pregnant. When we went out for dinner with our parents and spouses, Janet asked my father if he was happy he had children.

"The race hasn't been run yet," he replied without hesitation. His primary rule of repartee was "better never than late," and for him, all conversation was repartee. In this case, however, he hadn't yet gathered enough information to make an informed decision; and he didn't want to jump to a premature conclusion about such a weighty matter. What if Janet and I were to become cannibalistic serial killers, resulting in him being shunned at his golf club?

We never had a dog or other pet because they were "useless appendages to modern society." As he was an accountant, everything for him came down to numbers. When, for example, I'd come back from a movie, he had only one question: "What percentage of the seats were filled?"

When not working, he read or played golf or cards, leaving my mother to make her own life, which was fine with her since she was unusually self-absorbed. Although their marriage worked well for them (they were gifted with the lack of desire to examine their lives—maybe they got that from me), they served as terrible role models for a healthy, happy long-term relationship between a man and a woman or, for that matter, two or more people identifying as one or more of the newly discovered genders. Even under the best of circumstances, such relationships are rare as rocking horse shit, although people blessed with the gift of self-deception believe otherwise. Still, had I known fifty-five years ago what I now know about women, I'd have devised more creative and amusing ways to fuck up my relationships.

My father carried in his wallet a list of dozens of punch lines written in infinitesimal script.

"I haven't seen your joke list for a while," I said at another family dinner not long after I graduated from law school.

"Didn't you hear they stole it?" My mother's tone conveyed her horror at civilization's loss, surely on par with the destruction of the

Library of Alexandria, the inundation of Atlantis, or the Taliban's annihilation of Buddha statues in the Bamiyan Valley.[2]

Turned out that *they'd* stolen his wallet, never knowing that *they* had purloined something more valuable than cash. At least Dad hadn't kept irreplaceable photos of Janet or me in his wallet.

My father gave me invaluable advice: Work: "A law firm is a hundred nice guys who, put together, make one big bastard." Kindness: "When you turn around after doing someone a favor, run like hell so they don't have a chance to kick you in the ass." Women: "Humor is death to romance," "Women don't have a sense of humor," and "Avoid exceptionally good-looking women because they'll always be admiring themselves in the mirror." I knew little of his dating life before he met my mother other than that he went out with the first Miss Subways, whom he'd met while his friend was getting a manicure at the Waldorf. Also, he often said something about casting your bread upon the waters and having it come back as raisin cake, but I never understood what that meant.

Although self-controlled and undemonstrative, Dad often cried in movies. When I was twelve, he took me to see *Exodus*. I was terrified that something was terribly wrong with him when I looked over and saw him sobbing when Paul Newman and Eva Marie Saint were taping closed the mouths of infants so they wouldn't cry as they were secretly escaping from their kibbutz on the eve of an attack by the Arabs.

I visited him a few years before he died. As I was leaving, he hugged me. *Wait, what?* Had it suddenly occurred to him that that was what normal fathers do? Was he trying to make up for decades

---

[2] As this autobiography proceeds and I become more confident, I hope to eschew pretentious references and the use of obscure words such as *eschew*.

of denying me affection? Was it a sign of approaching dementia? Could it even have been a spontaneous loving gesture? I was too stunned and confused to ask.

There came a time, of course, when it became too late to ask.

Christ, I'm tearing up as I write this.

My mother—Mimi to her friends and Miriam to my father— was an amateur artist who had the occasional show where she sold a few paintings. A private self-obsessed person, she prided herself on not talking about her kids. Suffering through several miscarriages, she didn't have a child (me) until she was twenty-nine—late for those days. And by then, she'd put up with years of her friends bragging about their children. As a result, she vowed that when she finally had children, she wouldn't brag about them. To play it safe, she refrained even from talking about Janet or me. I'm not sure her reaction made logical sense, but that was what she said. And thank God, we humans are not required to make logical sense, particularly when it comes to feelings, emotions, desires, *and* autobiographies.

When I'd tell my mother I was unhappy, she'd respond, "So? Who's happy?" I inherited from her the shit-colored glasses through which I now view the world. That point of view will undoubtedly taint this autobiography. But every string of spoken or written words, including those composed by AI, is tainted by the point of view of the composer. Read on for more self-serving rationalizations.

When she read a novel I wrote,[3] which was published to some praise albeit miniscule sales, she declared it wasn't her "cup of tea."

---

[3] For a good time, read *girl*, available on Amazon. See www.robertnchan.com. While it might not be your cup of tea, it could well be your cocktail shaker of martinis. All royalties go to charity—the care and feeding of yours truly. However, I admit that they've barely been sufficient to keep me in cigarette money, which is disappointing since I don't smoke.

Her comment cut particularly deep since she drank coffee, so tea wasn't even her cup of tea.

Mom valued form over substance. For example, from the time I left for college, I, at her insistence, spoke on the phone with her and my dad every Sunday night. In those calls, however, she showed little interest in what I was doing or how I was feeling. If anything, she showed even less interest in Janet's life. Her favorite topic of conversation was herself—a trait a writer of an autobiography is hardly in a position to criticize.

Mom had been engaged to a man who'd been killed in World War II and met my father on the rebound. In her dotage, she'd insisted that she'd been married twice. I think she was trying to confess, or brag, to Janet and me that she hadn't been a virgin when she'd married my father—not that either of us felt the need to know that.

She always lied about, or more often adamantly refused to reveal, her age, even when my son, Adam (who, as a little boy, was obsessed with numbers and math), would ask her. A devoted Yankees fan, she was written up in the *New York Times* sports section as one of the oldest Yankee fans. On the strength of that article, when the old Yankee Stadium was about to be decommissioned, WPIX, which broadcasted some of the games, invited us to the stadium and did a segment on her. There, she whispered to Hall of Fame reliever Goose Gossage, "I never tell anyone my age, but I'll tell you. I'm ninety-five." Her whisper, however, was as loud as one's normal speaking voice. So the entire viewing audience heard it. The stadium was also the scene of one of her proudest moments that year: I took her to a game, and the concessionaire demanded to see her ID before selling her a beer.

Friendly and outgoing, she always talked to strangers, particularly men, which made me uncomfortable when I was young and the men uncomfortable when she got older. When Dad was suffering from Parkinson's-related dementia and Mom was in her eighties, he had an affable young Black man as an aide, who became a good friend of Mimi's. She felt compelled to tell us they weren't having sex.

In her early nineties, she regularly ended up in the emergency room due to falls resulting from running with her walker to make a bus, rushing to cross a street before the light turned, or shunning the elevator and taking the escalator because elevators are for the disabled, elderly, or infirm. Lying about her age had become so habitual that she'd even lied to herself about it. Just the same, she was tough and resolute and wouldn't let infirmity slow her down.

She had the bad luck to live until ninety-nine, long after all her friends had shuffled off this mortal coil. Lonely, bored, and confined to a wheelchair, but still mentally all there, she hated being dependent on round-the-clock caregivers. She repeatedly told me I shouldn't feel bad when she died as she was ready to "pop off." So when she passed away after a short illness, which a few years earlier she'd have shrugged off, I accepted her death with something approaching equanimity. If she was okay with dying, I should've been too. But not being made of her stern stuff, I wasn't. She died just before the onslaught of COVID. Janet and I were thankful she hadn't had to endure the isolation that living through the plague would have required and would, to her, have been literally a fate worse than death.

I loved my mother and miss her. While she could have been more supportive and affectionate, I'm sure she loved me to the best of her ability.

I fear that I've conveyed the wrong impression of my parents. In balance, they were better than most. They were generous and never abusive. They just weren't affectionate. I can't remember either of them ever telling me they loved me; and except for the hugging incident with my dad described above, hugs, kisses, and even tender touching were virtually nonexistent. If I'd have confronted my mom on that issue, she'd have claimed not to know what I was talking about, and I'm sure she wouldn't have. Confident that she loved me, she saw no reason to show it.

Hating pretense and phonies, Dad mistrusted all displays and words of affection, believing only actions counted—apparently to him, hugs and kisses weren't actions. Dutiful to a fault, he made sure that neither my mother, Janet, nor I suffered from material want; and to him, that was enough. Never having been materialistic, we didn't ask for much. But whatever Janet or I wanted within reason, they gave us, including gladly paying for college and, in my case, law school. Also, they gave me remarkably little guidance, never, for example, pushing me to excel at school or anything else.

I wonder why, when I try to accurately and dispassionately set out the facts of my life, it ends up sounding like I have a massive chip on my shoulder, which, believe me, I don't. Maybe it has something to do with those feces-colored glasses. Yeah, when someone says "believe me," that's the last thing you should do. But hey, I'm not just someone—I'm your beloved autobiographer. Okay, *beloved* is a step too far. Perhaps *not yet actively despised* is more accurate.

To provide a fuller picture of my background, I must go backward before moving forward. In 1898, at the age of twelve, my maternal grandfather, Herman Nelson, left Poland (then part of Russia, although he always referred to it as Poland, a country whose geographic existence had been snuffed out in the 1795 Third

Partition) on foot to avoid the spreading pogroms and the twenty-five years of servitude that the Imperial Russian Army had been imposing on Jewish children as young as twelve. Reaching Holland, he stowed away on a steamer to London,[4] where he joined up with his older brother, Philip, who was eking out a living as a prizefighter. They eventually made it to the Lower East Side of Manhattan, where they shared a room with eighteen other immigrants. Ten of them slept in that room during the day, and the other ten used it at night. Every Sabbath, Philip (who died before I was born) and Herman treated themselves to a wheel of cheese on which, along with scraps of several-days-old bread, they subsisted for the week. Through the mutual aid society formed by immigrants from their town in the Pale, he met and then married my grandmother Francis.

By 1925, the two brothers owned a business—the Nelson Bead Company, which they referred to as the Place—that imported glass and ceramic beads and crystals that they used to fabricate chandeliers. Herman owned a Pierce-Arrow, resided in an apartment on Central Park West, and had a summer bungalow in Long Beach, Long Island. Then came the Depression and World War II—bad times for Jews in the business of importing from Poland and Czechoslovakia. From 1930 on, he, Francis, and their children (Mimi, Gloria, and Irwin) lived a precarious existence. Moving frequently to take advantage of the months of free rent offered by Depression landlords, they couldn't even afford a dress for my mother to wear to her high school graduation. The business recovered somewhat in the '50s, allowing my grandparents to live

---

[4] He always insisted that Nelson was a Polish name and not one he took when residing in England as perhaps a homage to Horatio Nelson of the famous column. Also, according to the internet, the Russian army had ceased conscripting Jewish children in 1857. But who are you going to believe, Google or my sainted grandfather? In any event, the pogroms provided sufficient motivation to flee.

in insecure middle-class comfort. Perhaps her family's precarious situation when she was growing up and the cultural knowledge of the anti-Jewish pogroms from which her parents had fled had stamped themselves on Mom's psyche. Perhaps not. Like most things, it's hard to know. Both my parents lived by the adage "Expect the worst, and you'll rarely be disappointed." As a result, they were disappointed before they had reason to be.

Francis, who doted on me, had a fatal heart attack on a city bus, several weeks after my bar mitzvah. Lonely and embittered, Herman lived another three years, dying after spending his last dollar.

Other than my father, my role model was Uncle Irwin, who'd flown bombers in World War II and the Korean War. He was terrific with children. We'd wrestle with him. Unlike the more competitive Herman, he always let us win, and we'd joyfully pretend to shoot him with antiaircraft cannon. However, paranoid and susceptible to conspiracy theories, he couldn't get along with adults. He was the one who, when I was too young to properly process the information, told me about my mother's first engagement to, according to him, the love of her life. He repeatedly pulled stunts like buying Janet and me a cute puppy, knowing our parents wouldn't let us keep a dog. Once, he showed up at a Passover seder with a wheelchair, telling my grandfather that that was where he'd end up if he kept smoking, then getting into a knife fight with Larry, his brother-in-law and my aunt Gloria's husband.[5] By the time I was in high school, he'd alienated himself from our entire family and most everyone else.

---

[5] The scheming, troublemaking Gloria eventually divorced Larry, who replaced her and their preternaturally despicable daughter, Leanne, with a pet monkey, which was unquestionably an upgrade.

My father's parents, Max and Bertha Chan, emigrated from Cologne and Vienna, respectively, and thought of themselves as more German than Jewish. Orderly, unemotional, and taciturn, they considered affection to be a sign of weakness. When my parents were first engaged, Herman and Francis invited them to their Passover seder, where Bertha held forth on the silly superstitions, ridiculous myths, and meaningless empty rituals that underlie the holiday and the religion in general—an example of how the less religious German Jews generally looked down on the more religious Eastern European ones. Most of Bertha's and Max's relatives, also proud of their Germanness, had remained in Europe, only to be murdered in the Holocaust. Turned out that Hitler considered them more Jewish than German.

Barring twice-a-year visits, we had little to do with my father's side of the family, seeing as my father didn't get along with his brother and considered family to be a source of obligation and not pleasure.

My father's brother's three children, my cousins, were extremely intelligent, but, in the opinion of my parents, "a little off." I liked Alan, who was a year younger than me. After being an academic star at the prestigious Bronx High School of Science, he went to MIT, where he studied engineering and applied mathematics. He, however, dropped out well before obtaining a degree and moved back in with his parents, where he lived in his childhood room with a girl who had the habit of walking around the house naked, which rattled my aunt and uncle. He supported himself by selling weed from their Jackson Heights, Queens, semidetached home; and his parents struggled not to understand what was going on when youngsters showed up at odd hours and left shortly thereafter carrying small paper bags. Eventually, he moved to the

Pacific Northwest and made it big in the administration of Dianetics, Scientology, and their offshoots. I also liked his sisters: Rita, a lesbian beatnik who became a psychotherapist in San Francisco, and Marylin, a very pretty left-leaning high school teacher. They, however, were older than me. So regretfully I didn't have much of a relationship with either.

My sister, Janet, was—and surprisingly enough still is—four years younger than me. All our parents demanded of us was that we didn't fight. Accordingly, they discouraged us from playing together. To this day, Janet seems to resent that I wasn't a better big brother. But what did I know? I was a kid just following orders—perhaps an infelicitous phrase.

More than two decades ago, after a huge Thanksgiving fight (although I don't remember the details—I'm sure she does and that it was entirely my fault), I asked my sister to breakfast to talk things through. There, she said, "I love you, but I don't like you." Since then, knowing she dislikes me and seeing that she always puts the most negative spin conceivable on everything I do and say, I've been uncomfortable around her. There have been numerous subsequent misunderstandings that she'd likely characterize as *understandings*. Janet also resented that when our mom's health was deteriorating, more of the burden of her care fell on her. She had a point—although I was working at the time, and she wasn't. Besides, Mom, who preferred men to women, thought caring for her was woman's work not appropriate for her firstborn son.

A pity as I like Janet, as does most everyone who knows her; and I particularly like my brother-in-law, Tyler. Amy, my wife, and I are quite fond of Janet's kids—my niece and nephew, whom we rarely get a chance to see. I'm something of a mixed bag; and Amy, like all of us, isn't perfect. But it would be hard to find a kinder, more loving aunt than Amy.

Tyler, Amy, and I go out for dinner from time to time, which is generally pleasant despite my sister's passive-aggressive undertone. Janet, Tyler, and I took frequent walks together during COVID, which I enjoyed and appreciated. Yet her imparting the most sinister interpretation to everything I do or say continues to hurt. See, contrary to what some have said, I have feelings, although precious little good they've done me.

As you'll see, I have many good friends and am well-liked, even if I may be an acquired taste like oysters, haggis, or anchovies. I'd say I'm likable once people get to know me, but Janet has had more of a chance to get to know me than anyone else on earth. Maybe the sweet spot of my likability comes when people get to know me somewhat, but not all that well.

In seventh grade, curious to see what it would be like to be in an actual fistfight, I punched a classmate in the face. The next day, his mother drove him to my house so he could get revenge. In those days, bullying—like infectious diseases[6]—was considered an essential part of the childhood experience. When I told my mother that my year-older neighbor, David Herman, periodically beat me up, she said, "Hit him back." It didn't seem to matter to her and wouldn't have mattered to most parents in those days, that he was bigger and stronger than me. Getting one's ass kicked was

---

[6] If there had been a COVID plague then, people would have gone on with their lives—or deaths—without giving it much thought. My parents' generation never tired of telling us that they'd survived the Great Depression and won World War II. COVID has already killed twice the number of Americans who died in that war, but never mind. Polio, the plague of those years, didn't cause anyone to lose a step other than, of course, those whom it paralyzed.

believed to build character and teach kids their appropriate place in a capitalistic society. It didn't work for me. I've generally felt out of place in society; and as for character, let's just say, "The race hasn't been run yet."

Once we reached junior high, David and I became best friends. We spent most Saturday nights playing Ping-Pong and darts in my basement, where we guzzled Hawaiian punch and giggled over stupid jokes. Indeed, it was their stupidity that made them funny. Once, he laughed so long and hard that he passed out from a lack of oxygen. Although he now lives in California, we talk weekly; and he comes to New York several times a year, mostly on business, never failing to call and get together with me.

In eighth grade, a new boy in our class threw a party where the boys were supposed to bring dates—yikes! I figured I couldn't go wrong by inviting the cutest, most talented, and most sophisticated girl in my class, Teri Sue Feldshuh—subsequently a successful actress under the name Tovah Feldshuh. In class photos, she looked like a woman surrounded by children, as if she were Snow White and we kids were the Twenty-Five Dwarfs. Of course, it could've gone wrong if she'd rejected me, which any objective observer would have believed to be the most likely result. She, however, accepted. A good actress even then, she appeared to be enthusiastic about going with me, and maybe she really was. How would I know?

Once at the party, I had no idea what to do. So I hung out in one corner with the other clueless boys. She hung with the girls. When two kids split off and started necking, she commented favorably to me. That hint, unsubtle though it was, was too subtle for my terrified unformed mind to grasp. In retrospect, my failure to take her up on her implicit offer was a missed opportunity. Not a consequential one, however. She was too much woman for me—part of a pattern that would emerge in my tortuous search for love.

If this were a typical autobiography, I'd lay bare the deep and profound feelings I had about this and each subsequent event. However, other than knowing that my feelings were neither deep nor profound, I don't remember how I felt about it—one of several advantages of the unexamined life. Although the psychiatric establishment would disagree, it seems to me that the less one thinks about negative feelings, the less one feels them. Indeed, I fear that as I proceed with this autobiography, I'll increasingly get in touch with my suppressed feelings. Hopefully, I'll succeed in keeping them at bay with attempts at humor. That tried-and-true technique has worked for me over the years, but as they say in the investment industry, "past performance is no guarantee of future results."

II

High School Confidential

1962–1964 (and drifting a little into 1968)

One evening, sophomore year, I was desultorily doing geometry proofs while watching *The Many Loves of Dobie Gillis* and lusting after a young Tuesday Weld. By then, I knew what to do if Ms. Weld were to suggest we make out, even if much of what might follow from there was still fuzzy. I figured, though, that if that were ever to happen, she'd guide me through the process. I was certain that underneath her bitchy exterior, she was a sexy little angel and would make an excellent girlfriend. Disappointingly, she never called. But that evening, my best friend, Peter, did. "I just did something you've never done," he said. We'd used that phrase to introduce disclosures of momentous events, such as when I claimed to have reached third base with a girl, even if, technically, I'd made it to second standing up and had been called out trying to steal.

He paused for effect. Anticipatory jealousy roiled in my stomach. Nothing, though, could've prepared me for what I was about to hear.

"I smoked pot," he declared.

I'd heard that beatniks and Negroes did that, and disturbingly, Peter's older brother at Williams also partook. But Peter being so foolishly self-destructive? After all, marijuana wouldn't have been illegal if it weren't harmful. Appalled, perplexed, and profoundly shaken (hey, these are some genuine feelings), I turned to the repository of all knowledge. The *Encyclopedia Americana* described *cannabis* as "a nonaddictive intoxicant producing a sense of euphoria." *Euphoria* sounded good, and as Voltaire said, "Once a philosopher twice a pervert." So in search of metaphysical truth and with no intention of indulging in a perversion that could lead to my lying in a gutter, a hypodermic needle hanging limply from my arm, skin ash gray, white foam bubbling from my lips, I'd try it just once.

Not seeing the blinding white light or having achieved even an iota of enlightenment, I tried weed again and then again, as would any intellectually curious philosopher or, for that matter, any dull-witted pervert. Maybe I wasn't doing it right. Eventually, I decided I enjoyed uncontrollable giggling, coining brilliant-sounding turns of phrase, experiencing the music behind the music, and discovering the extraordinary nutritional value of raw cookie dough. Sure, I risked arrest and a deathly descent into hard drugs, but balancing the pros and cons . . . Fuck it, you should know me well enough by now to realize I wouldn't have spent a nanosecond doing such balancing. The pros were sufficient to obviate any consideration of the cons.

Also, marijuana was superior to the alternative high. There would be no repeats of the time when, having driven home drunk, I dropped a half-empty bottle of Old Mr. Boston premixed screwdrivers on the garage floor. Too shit-faced to clean it up but not wanting my parents to drive over the shards of glass, I scrawled a note: "I dropped a bottle I was holding for a friend on the garage floor. Will clean it up in the morning." "Holding for a friend"? No matter, I cleaned up the glass in the morning, and my parents never mentioned the incident. Lucky for me, they weren't in touch with their feelings and didn't feel compelled to express those they failed to suppress. Unlike today's helicopter parents, they were foxhole parents or maybe hiding-in-a-bunker parents. They believed in letting me make my own mistakes, and I was only too happy to accommodate them.

Several years later, when I was home from college for summer vacation, some pals[7] and I had been sitting on my bedroom floor for hours, smoking weed. We were gathered around an upside-down trash can that served as the base of a water pipe I'd made from lab equipment I'd *liberated* from a chemistry lab. Zoned out, we were vacantly gazing at a light box device I'd invented using blinking Christmas lights and indirect lighting plastic panels. *Sgt. Pepper's Lonely Hearts Club Band* played on my record player, volume turned high, while Motown blasted from a tape recorder.

Having come home earlier than expected, my mother materialized in my bedroom, image distorted by the haze of smoke. My stoned friends gasped. One who periodically suffered from a collapsed lung began loudly hyperventilating. Mom said, "Bobby dear, please turn down the music. Dad and I are going to bed." The next morning, neither of my parents said a word about the incident. Like talented actors, my parents never broke character.

Somewhat ahead of the curve, I smoked weed in high school. So what? Point is, it transformed my worldview. If what the authorities said about pot was so off base, what about the rest of what they said? Maybe, for example, the greatest country in the world shouldn't be destroying villages in Southeast Asia in order to save them, like how during the Inquisition, Jews, Muslims, and other heretics were burned at the stake to save their souls. Smoking

---

[7] One friend was my fraternity brother Mark Phillips, of the hugely successful Phillips Collection, who recently promised to buy multiple copies of this autobiography if I mentioned him. Mark, how's that for product placement?

dope and the concomitant lawbreaking affected many of my generation, but that didn't make the experience any less significant for me. *People try to put us d-down (Talkin' 'bout my generation) / Just because we get around (Talkin' 'bout my generation)...* Oh, never mind.

The late '60s and early '70s were exciting years—how glorious to be a soldier on the front lines of the "sex, drugs, and rock 'n' roll" revolution. Much of what we did played out on the cover of *Time* magazine and on the TV news, including the canonical *CBS Nightly News with Walter Cronkite.* That conferred an undeserved legitimacy to our fads, quarter-baked beliefs, and peculiar styles of dress and hygiene. Those times, however, have passed; and the aged hippies who've maintained the habits and values of those times, although the nicest of people, have been swept up into the dustbin of history.

My generation's naive, sophomoric, self-indulgent narcissism hasn't stood the test of time. It was, however, much more fun than the current generation's arrogant, dreary, judgmental cancel culture, which is indifferent to actual culture and obsessed with rooting out the most insignificant mini microaggressions while freely committing macroaggressions against Jews. Oh shit! I may have just alienated an entire generation of potential book buyers. Nah, due to their inability to focus for more than the length of a TikTok video, they don't read anything longer than a tweet.

A little harsh and overstated? Sure, but I'm pandering to my potential baby-boomer readers who feel the same way as I do but are too sensible to put it in writing. Also, if any youngsters have read this far, they've already bought the book, so fuck 'em.

III

Dirty Tricks

1965–1966

I didn't know many ambitious kids, but even if I'd known thousands, Jimmy still would've been the most ambitious. One of his proudest moments was when he broke the arm of a rival so he could supplant the boy as quarterback of the grade school football team. It's possible his story might not actually have been true, but if he'd made it up, it would have been even worse in a way. On the other hand, the dominant one, he laughed at my jokes, thereby clearing the low bar to being my friend. Also, as he thought he could use me to his advantage, I cleared his low bar. I didn't like him much, but that didn't matter as no one else did either.

Jimmy's mother constantly belittled his father, an unsuccessful small-town lawyer who'd graduated from Lehigh. Nothing shameful in that. Indeed, it was one of the few colleges I'd visited with my father (golf season had ended, and tax season had not yet started, so spending time with me wasn't an onerous imposition as long as we didn't have to drive more than two hours away from home). There, I was favorably impressed by the condom machines in the bathroom of the greasy spoon, near the campus, in which we'd had lunch. Jimmy's mother, though, thought she'd married beneath her intellectually and financially. Ambitious as her son (the poisoned apple rarely falls far from the tree), she decreed that Jimmy must go to Harvard as a first step in the tortuous process of erasing the family stain.

As Jimmy and his mother conceived it, the path to Harvard ran through the presidency of the student council. Over cooking sherry he and I had purloined from his mom's kitchen cabinet, he disclosed their plan to me. Quite obviously, he wasn't going to ascend to the presidency on popularity. Therefore, he needed someone like me to be his campaign manager, chief of oppo research, and dirty tricks officer; and I was the only one like me he knew.

"Why would I want to do that?" I asked.

"It would be a good college credential."

"I doubt that being your campaign manager would whisk me into the Ivy League."

"When elected, I'll appoint you to a plum position in student government."

"What's the second prize, an enema with a fire hose?"

College was two years away, and I assumed it would take care of itself. After all, I'd gotten into public elementary school, middle school, and high school without any effort; and I was really smart even if I'd yet to demonstrate my superior intelligence to anyone but myself.

"It'll be a good way to meet freshman and sophomore girls," he said.

"I'm in."

My first official duty was to attend a meeting with the principal, the candidates, and the campaign managers. The principal talked us through the byzantine campaign rules—my first experience with the inverse relationship between the importance of an endeavor and the complexity of its rules. When the principal reached the part about school lists, I roused myself from erotic fantasies about the hot girls I intended to put on my committee and what they'd do to show their appreciation.[8] Each campaign would be issued one, and it had to be guarded like the nails from the True Cross. Possession of a second list or copying the list would result in expulsion from the race. He explained that one of the reasons they were so tightly guarded was that mailing list companies would pay to get their hands on a compilation of the phone numbers and addresses of all Scarsdale High students and their parents.

Picking up on what I interpreted as an implicit hint, I sold a copy to such a company, clearing $480—big money for me at the time. The principal's admonitions also inspired a scheme by which I could overcome Jimmy's likability deficit.

The high school printing club's ostensible purpose was to print signs announcing events, tickets to such events, and the like. Its most useful role, however, was printing Bermuda draft cards to be used as proof that we were over the drinking age. I never saw anyone over eighteen at our bar of choice, the Candlelight, a place so dingy that the name must've been intended ironically, like a giant nicknamed Tiny. Over time, the bartender probably developed a skewed idea of what eighteen-year-olds, or at least Bermudan eighteen-year-olds, looked like.

The Candlelight watered down their drinks, perhaps especially for Bermuda draft card holders. All the sweeteners in our drinks of choice, however, would have given us a sugar high. It took three Singapore slings and a bourbon sour for me to convince the

---

[8] These days, in conformance with the current zeitgeist, I, like most every other male, pretend that my thoughts are as pure as those of a lobotomized eunuch. But then, with the #MeToo movement five decades in the future, I could have such thoughts without guilt, particularly as there was no chance that they'd come to fruition.

campaign manager for the leading candidate, to plant copies of school lists in the lockers of Jimmy's freshman and sophomore campaign managers, after which he'd file a complaint with the principal, alleging copying and misusing of the lists, and Jimmy would be ejected from the race. Not only did I sell this guy on the play, but also I convinced him that he had come up with it—a negotiating ploy that would serve me well in future years.

Closing the trap on the gullible campaign manager by catching him in the act of planting the lists wasn't hard. All it took was a stakeout staffed with Jimmy's supporters. When caught, he confessed to having done it to help Jimmy's opponent, thereby making the case that Jimmy's opponent was involved in prohibited dirty tricks. The hard part was managing the ensuing crisis by playing on the principal's fear that even the most inconsequential scandals at the iconic Scarsdale High School would find their way to the front page of the *New York Times*. His initial reaction was to ignore the incident. But once I arranged for Jimmy to threaten to resign (guaranteeing a public scandal that would likely be reported on page B-1 of the *Times*, but below the fold), he had no choice other than to ask the leading candidate to resign. Being a class act, unlike Jimmy, he did so graciously.

Sure, I knew that helping Jimmy pad his college application to the detriment of the more qualified candidate was, at best, ethically questionable. I, however, had constructed a rationalization: student government was a farce. Whether Jimmy or his opponent served as school president was irrelevant to the students' welfare, and therefore, my dirty tricks caused no harm in the real world. It wasn't until I'd been practicing law for a few years that I realized that humans have an unlimited capacity for rationalization and self-righteousness. Indeed, almost every client I ever had honestly and sincerely believed himself to be not just in the right but standing next to God when he said, "Let there be light." Of course, even as a high school junior, I should've known that my rationalization was self-serving crapola. But as Upton Sinclair said, "It is difficult to get a man to understand something, when his salary depends on his not understanding it." For socially insecure teenage boys, the opportunity to meet attractive girls is the functional equivalent of the salary a working person depends on to feed his or her family. Pretty good rationalization, right? Well, maybe not. Now with the benefit of my elite legal training, I could come up with better.

Not one to make waves or even ripples that might dampen his anticipated college recommendations, Jimmy made no effort to change or improve anything for fear of antagonizing someone in the administration. As chairman of the election board, the plummiest of supposedly plum positions, I rewrote the rules to make dirty tricks more difficult. I also staffed the board with the prettiest girls, not that they showed their appreciation—although they might have if I'd been sufficiently self-confident to ask them out.

Yeah, I know, that doesn't sound great. But even from the point of view of today's #MeToo vigilantes, my conduct wouldn't have risen to even the low level of a mini microaggression. The most militant of culture warriors have yet to cancel people for aberrant thoughts. Sure, that might be coming, unless Trump beats them to the punch by sending communists, socialists, Democrats, and RINOs to reeducation camps. Gee, it's difficult to write an honest autobiography and not offend anybody. Luckily, I don't give a shit. On second thought, actually, I do. Please, someone, anyone, cancel me! It'll help book sales. Indeed, that's likely my only hope. Maybe I should hire a cadre of young leftists to picket in front of my building and then hire a PR maven to notify MSNBC and Fox.

I was the shortest boy in my class, but as a kid, I didn't give the matter much thought. Not only did I strive to keep such thinking to a minimum, but also I was generally well-liked and respected—certainly more so than Jimmy. My mother wanted me to get growth hormone shots, but to my subsequent regret, I declined. My father was short, and I admired him more than anybody. Jimmy, though, made it his mission to draw my attention to my lack of stature, repeatedly questioning why I didn't have an inferiority complex or a Napoleonic need to overcompensate. Ultimately, he succeeded in making me conscious of my height, adding to my insecurity, and perhaps installing in me a need to overcompensate and destroy my enemies in my personal battle of Austerlitz. Great! I just realized that I have someone other than myself to blame for my neuroses since it has occurred to me that it's unseemly to blame my dearly departed parents.

In the summer between junior and senior years in high school, Jimmy and I went to Europe on the pretext of studying French, which never actually happened—*cela n'est jamais réellement arrivé.* A self-styled sophisticated man of the world, Jimmy was intent on getting me laid. I was unenthusiastic as paying for sex didn't conform to my romantic fantasies, yet it seemed unmanly to demur.

On the first night in Paris, we strolled the Champs-Élysées, where Jimmy had it on good authority that hookers hung out. Any unaccompanied women we saw could have purchased us many times over had they wanted to, not that any of them even glanced in our direction. The next night, taking a more down-market approach, Jimmy led me down a poorly lit side street off another side street in Montmartre, where we saw a bar with a red neon sign: Le Bar Suzie.

"This is it," Jimmy assured me.

"How do you know?"

He responded with a condescending eyebrow raise.

Sure enough, there were two women alone at the bar. Not unattractive, I supposed. But at sixteen, I was attracted to girls but intimidated by women.

We took seats at the bar, and Jimmy flirted with them in demure, stilted high-school French. They didn't flirt back. Either they didn't know they were being flirted with or considered doing nothing preferable to conversing with a self-important underage twerp and his mute underling. In a gesture of studied grandiloquence, Jimmy handed the bartender a $20 bill to tack on the wall alongside the various small-denomination franc, mark, and lira notes already pasted there.

I thought engaging prostitutes would have been a straightforward process, but he assured me that the situation required Japanese-tea-ceremony-like obeisance to recondite rules and customs that he, although only a rising high school senior, was somehow privy to. Then two menacing muscular men emerged from a back room and communicated nonverbally that it was past our bedtimes.

On the third night, we went to a strip joint—an unthreatening, titillating entertainment that I quite enjoyed. After that, the Metro having shut down for the night, we took a cab back to our hotel.

Jimmy explained to the driver in even more bombastic French than usual that we were the sons of the Swiss ambassador—me being his sheltered borderline-retarded younger brother. He chose that pose because he didn't want to trigger the driver's unexpressed, but surely latent, anti-Americanism. It didn't seem to occur to him that the driver would wonder why a Swiss ambassador's child would have a strong American accent. It took Jimmy some time to get to the point—or rather to circle around the point and sneak up to it from behind. Given who we were, we were loath to cause an international incident. Therefore, we needed to know where lowlifes, criminals, and prostitutes hung out so we could avoid going there.

The taxi came to a tire-screeching halt.

"Ah, you want to fuck," the driver said. "I'll show you a place where you can fuck like ze king." His use of ze, rather than the, was intended to inject local color as his English was at least a match of Jimmy's French.

He took us to a fin de siècle town house, rang the bell, and handed us off to a maternal woman with a thickly painted and cratered face like an overripe peach. She sat us in an over-furnished, Second Empire, manqué parlor room and yanked a velvet bellpull. Women in lingerie arrayed themselves on a spiral staircase. Because of my inability to speak the language, but more because he liked to lord his superiority over me, Jimmy picked one for me. While I'd rather have chosen for myself, he didn't do badly by me. But she was definitely a woman, not a girl, and one I couldn't communicate with in my native and only tongue. She led me to a room, undressed, and bid me to do the same. I'd never been with a naked woman, and the situation was aesthetically pleasing . . . but too intimidating to be arousing. I'd imagined the process would entail being with someone I liked, could talk to, and perhaps flirt with to the limited extent I knew how to. We'd begin with necking and move on from there. This was all too . . . something. But whatever it was, it wasn't arousing.

As if reading my mind, she asked if I would like a kiss.

"Very much."

I puckered my lips.

She went down on me.

At any other time, in any other situation, that would have been the turn-on it would become in later years. But this time, in this situation, it was . . . wilting and embarrassing.

By the time we returned to New York, Jimmy and I were no longer friends.

The student council presidential election front-runner got into Harvard without the hassle of having to serve as president. Perhaps due to the principal's blackball, however, Jimmy was rejected everywhere and had to use his father's pull to weasel his way into Lehigh. From there, he went to law school and married his high school girlfriend, whom he'd wooed because she was the daughter of the managing partner of a top Wall Street law firm. Joining that firm and exploiting his father-in-law's contacts,[9] he reached such an exalted level of success that, when he was fired for sexual harassment years later, the story made the front page of both the *New York Law Journal* and the *Wall Street Journal*—above the fold.

Senior year in high school was one of the happiest years of my life. Getting my driver's license liberated me. I had many friends as well as acquaintances who seemed to be friends until we graduated, and we immediately lost touch with each other. More to the point, I had a hot girlfriend, with daring fashion-forward blond streaks in her hair. With access to a car; I was free to go wherever I wanted, with anyone I wanted, particularly as my parents showed little interest in what I did.

Although my high school classmates were obsessed with getting into the most prestigious colleges they could manage, I still hadn't given the matter much thought; and my parents saw no reason to involve themselves in the process, beyond my trip to Lehigh with my

---

[9] He claimed he'd interviewed with many of the major firms and chose the best. It was a total coincidence that his father-in-law happened to run the place. Unlike cliché-plagued TV detectives, I believe in coincidences, but not that one.

dad. A classmate spent a weekend with his cousin at the University of Michigan. They smoked marijuana, and a girl slept over in his cousin's dorm room. I knew a little something about weed and just enough about sex to know I wanted to learn a lot more about both. Also, the Playmate of the Month had posed in a frat house at the University of Illinois, and I figured Illinois and Michigan were interchangeable. I applied to Michigan and, due to rolling admissions, got in, in three weeks: problem solved before it had even become a problem. Years later, my mother insisted that I'd chosen U of M because I wanted to go to a school with a good football team—a consideration that hadn't even crossed my mind. If she'd actually believed that at the time, one would've thought she'd have advised me that that wasn't the ideal criterion in choosing where to go to college. But she prided herself on not interfering.

IV

Frat Bro

1966–1968

Like the Jewish frat in *Animal House*, my fraternity (also a Jewish one) had the highest grade point average on campus—my first choice had been the coolest Jewish frat, but they weren't smart enough to recognize my essential coolness. Reflecting the changing times, my frat contained two distinct coexisting tribes: the alcohol-swilling, politically conservative Barbarians, and the drug-taking, politically radical Self-Righteous Brothers.

For the annual Florida Party, we all contributed cash to a fund and went with our dates to the airport, where we'd draw out of a hat the name of the lucky winner. He and his date would get a long weekend in Florida—a welcome break from the Michigan winter—and the rest of us would return to the frat house and get shit-faced. In my sophomore year, in what was known as a *pimp job*, we fixed the lottery so one of the more barbaric Barbarians won a one-way flight to Fargo, North Dakota, along with a check to cover all expenses payable to Fuck Yourself. We hustled him and his date to the gate just as the plane was taking off so they wouldn't realize the actual destination until it was too late.

For the Barn Party, another highlight of the frat's social calendar, we covered the main floor of the frat house with straw;

rented a pig, a cow, and a few dozen chickens from a nearby farmer; and got hammered on Boone's Farm apple wine—one of whose ingredients was formaldehyde. One of my frat brothers kept a wastepaper basket lined with a plastic bag near his bed for when his girlfriend puked. Another went for a drive afterward and crashed his car into an automobile dealership parking lot, damaging eight cars—a fraternity record. Ah, tradition.

At least, unlike other frats, we were generally respectful of women and didn't fetishize alcohol, shoot horses upstairs in a third-floor bedroom so rigor mortis would make it impossible to remove the corpse without a buzz saw, or kidnap a passed-out brother and set him on an air mattress floating down the Huron River, colloquially known as the Urine. Oops, we actually did that one.

I majored in economics largely because I'd aced Economics 101 by barely cracking a book. Also, it was comforting to learn that achieving a full-employment productive economy was a simple matter of increasing governmental expenditures in times of slow growth and decreasing them when inflation started to heat up. If only economists ran the government.

Over the next couple of decades, however, economists gained more influence, and out of sheer perversity, the economy refused to conform to their theories.

In those days, psychedelics were a normal part of the college experience, at least for the more intellectually curious—that is, foolhardy. One slightly life-altering stoned insight: if a mere fifty micrograms of lysergic acid diethylamide-25 (a.k.a. LSD) could so completely transmogrify reality, maybe reality, as our senses perceived it, was more fluid than it had always seemed. That micro revelation led me to not take things—including my schoolwork and, subsequently, my early legal career—as seriously as I should have.

During one trip, I had a revelation, while huddling under a table at a fraternity mixer, that unhappiness and depression were mere states of mind and thus entirely within my control. Several weeks later, I found myself growing despondent, over a girl no doubt. I reminded myself of my revelation, but myself replied that my sadness was the appropriate response to what had happened. So much for that revelation.

This would be a good place for a hilarious story of an LSD trip. Too bad I don't remember any, or maybe there just weren't any amusing stories that could survive coming down from LSD into mundane reality. Oh wait, there was the time when my fraternity brother and close friend Michael and I dropped acid and drove to the Detroit Metropolitan Wayne County Airport to watch the planes land and, well, actually to offer rides home to attractive disembarking girls. No, that was more harrowing than hilarious; we barely survived all those flashing lights on the interstate intent on forcing us off the road to devour our brains and use our mental energy as an alternative source of power. Having not previously tried it, how were we to know that driving while tripping was a horrendous idea? At least I didn't drive drunk—not often anyway. For smart guys, we were astoundingly stupid. Or maybe for stupid guys, we were quite smart in our way.

As I've already admitted, we'd fallen for a whole lot of bullshit—transparent bullshit at that. But it was all new to us and fun and exciting to be part of that scene. I'd love to have some of those good times now. Hmm, maybe I should take a few tokes . . . Alas, weed no longer gives me giggle fits. Now it just makes me sleepy— and a bit horny, not that you or anyone else wants to hear about a seventy-five-year-old in that condition. So we'll quickly move along before that disgusting image embeds itself into your mind.

Between my junior and senior years in college, after working fourteen-hour days getting swimming pools ready for the summer, I hitched around Europe, mostly traveling alone since my fraternity brother/travel companion and I misplaced each other in Amsterdam, our first stop—with me going to London and him to Paris. We met again on the plane home.

As part of the trip, I spent several weeks sleeping on a beach under a star-filled sky on the far side of Mykonos, eating freshly grilled fish and drinking retsina at a beachside taverna, with a group of Swedes and Brits.[10] Each morning, I'd tell myself it was time to move on; and each night, I'd go to sleep, thinking what a wonderful day it had been.

Toward the end of the trip, I traveled with a guy I'd met on Mykonos, whose only comment on the St. Peter's Basilica, the Paris Catacombs, Hagia Sophia, and every other cultural monument we visited was "What a great place for a party."

On our flight back to New York, he had a kilo of Turkish hashish strapped to his lower back, which wasn't a cause for alarm since he had a plan. He'd persuaded a pixie-cute young woman, who looked as if she'd stepped out of a J.Crew catalog, to let him pose as her fiancé. Having gotten a conservative haircut and dressed in chinos, a blue button-down shirt, and a madras sport jacket, he looked the part of a preppy young man who'd never even try marijuana for fear that doing so would lead straight to psychosis,

---

[10] The difference between us Americans and Europeans who were hitching around on the cheap was that Europeans would partially support their travels by selling their blood. Brindisi and Thessaloníki were rumored to pay the most per liter.

heroin addiction, and excessive hair growth. It hadn't taken much effort on his part to convince her to help him because she needed him as much as he needed her. She was bringing back purchases valued at $200 more than the legal limit, and she wanted to avoid paying tariffs on that overage. He agreed to stow some of her swag in his suitcase and declare it in his name. The ruse worked . . . until the customs official said, "Good luck, son" and patted him on the small of his back, where he'd hidden the hash. They took him away in handcuffs, and I never saw nor heard from or about him again. I wonder if he thought the courtroom and prison would've been great places for a party.

V

Sally

1967–1968

I don't remember how I met Sally, the great love of my college years. My first recollection of being with her was when we were driving down Washtenaw Avenue, one of the main drags in Ann Arbor, with me at the wheel. She rhapsodized about how great cigarettes tasted after smoking weed. Never having smoked tobacco, I took a deep drag from her ciggy and held the smoke in, like I would've on a joint. Next thing I knew, I was coughing so hard I couldn't see or sit up, let alone drive. Before I finally regained a semblance of control, the car had swerved across the double white line to an angry cacophony of honking horns, then jumped a curb, almost taking out a mailbox and a trash bin. Laughing hysterically, she was of little help. I wasn't nearly as amused as she was. That incident should have raised a red flag, but Sally was the smartest woman I'd met up to that point. She'd charmed me with her poetic turns of phrase, unique worldview, and clever banter. Also, she was beautiful, cultured, sophisticated, and sexy in a way that seemed totally free of artifice, and somehow larger-than-life. Smitten, my mind transmogrified her reckless wildness into an erotic turn-on.

We flew to Washington to "storm the Pentagon"—one of the great late '60s antiwar protests. After we'd marched and chanted slogans long enough to develop an appetite, I suggested we enjoy a romantic lunch in a charming Georgetown restaurant. We couldn't end the Vietnam War, but we could enjoy an amorous meal. She, however, insisted on going where the tear gas was the thickest, where the soldiers with bayonets affixed to their M14s were subjected to the most harassment and accordingly were the most threatening, and where, if we got lucky, we'd get arrested, asphyxiated, or, even better, bayoneted. While choking and bleeding profusely from a stomach wound didn't sound to me like a good time, I was happy to be spending time with her. I persuaded myself that her zeal was grounded in political commitment and moral indignation rather than thrill-seeking foolhardiness.

On one of our last dates, she told me that, inspired by the Velvet Underground song "Heroin," she'd started shooting up but had stopped because it had become boring. She was too crazily willful to become addicted like a normal person. While I played at being a madcap risk-taker, deep down, I knew I was a poseur. She, though, wasn't playing.

Although she was appealing in so many ways, it subsequently occurred to me that what really got me going was that I never quite had her. At times, we were on the same wavelength, and I'd think she'd fallen for me as I had for her. The next day, however, or even the next hour, she'd become distant, as if our intense intimacy had taken place only in my imagination. The more unreachable she remained, while intermittently teasing me with the prospect of an intense relationship, the deeper I fell for her.[11] *Teasing* is the wrong

---

[11] B. F. Skinner, the father of behaviorism, demonstrated that random rewards, "intermittent reinforcement," are more effective than rewards offered on a regular schedule. Sally proved that the technique worked even better with sophomore boys as they were a breed hornier and more credulous than lab rats.

word as I never got a hint that she was playing games; she was just mercurial—a euphemism for *dangerously unstable*. Only in retrospect did it occur to me that a large part of my attraction to her was that her unavailability allowed me to preserve my fantasy of her without the unpleasant intrusion of reality—few fantasies can survive a relationship. I spent the latter half of my sophomore year nursing a broken heart, which contributed to making it one of my favorite years. Few things are more satisfying than being a romantic without having to struggle with an actual romance.

Years later, I ran into one of her ex-roommates in the Columbia Law School Library. She convinced me that rather than being a Delphic, poetic, and charming rebel, Sally was schizophrenic. Although able to function by dint of her brilliance, she was incapable of maintaining long-term or, for that matter, short-term relationships. Just the same, in my college years, if a girl was attractive, witty, and laughed at my attempts at humor, being crazy was not disqualifying any more than being a Red Sox fan or being unable to roll a compact joint. Anyway, I was right about her being authentic. Few people are more genuinely authentic than schizophrenics, not that authenticity is a positive characteristic in their cases. Wish I knew what finally became of her. Is she even still alive?

VI

You Say You Want a Revolution

1969

Ann Arbor, late sophomore year. Driving fast. Car radio blasting.

I'm disconsolate. Sally had torn out my heart with her teeth, soaked it in salt and Tabasco pepper sauce, stomped on it, replaced it lopsided, and sewn up my chest using rattlesnake fangs and vulture gut.

"Revolution" comes on. Having invested so much effort in being despondent, I don't want to sing along. That, however, is what one must do when the radio plays a new Beatles song.

Yeah, John, I'd said I *want a revolution*. But that's just what one says to fit in, to be hip. Yet I really do *want to change the world—* blow it the fuck up.

Don't you know it's gonna be all right? John Lennon sings.

No, in fact, I know it won't be.

Don't you know it's gonna be all right? I sing along.

John and I repeat the line as my singing morphs into screaming.

I run a red light on Washtenaw Avenue.

"All right, all right, all right, all right, all right!" I bellow.

Pedal to the metal, I run another light.

All right, all right, all right, all right, all right.

In an astounding alchemy only the Beatles can bring about, I suddenly know everything is gonna be all right.

Well, not actually *all right*. My heart is irreparably broken, but at least I know there'd be times when I'd hardly notice.

And the summer of 1969 presents numerous distractions for the young, hip, and befuddled.

VII

We Are Stardust, We Are Golden, and We've Got to Get Ourselves Back to the Garden

August 1969

"Fuck!" I slammed my fist on the dashboard. "I left our tickets home."

One hell of a time for me to realize that. For the past two hours, my three friends and I had been stuck in a twenty-mile traffic jam that stretched all the way back to the New York Thruway and down to the previous exit. We couldn't turn around and now had no reason to go forward.

My friends' silence was more upsetting than anything they could have said, but before I dissolved into a puddle of remorse and self-pity, we caught a lucky break.

A long-haired scalper tapped on our window and offered to sell us tickets. Since it was the Summer of Love, we were on the cusp of the Age of Aquarius, and we were all brothers and sisters; he charged us only a few bucks over the face value of the tickets. "I'm only making cigarette money," he said.

He, however, turned out to be a con hippie. The gargantuan crowd had torn down the security fences and, like Jesus casting out the money changers, driven off the ticket takers. The Woodstock

Music and Art Fair—a triumph of branding over truth as it took place forty miles from the actual Woodstock—was free to all.

By the time we got to Woodstock / We were half a million strong / And everywhere was a song / And a celebration. I could neither confirm nor deny the accuracy of Joni Mitchell's lyrics since by the time *we* got to Woodstock, we were so far from the stage that we couldn't see the performers and their music was reduced to a faint bassline accompanied by barely audible lyrics.

The prime spots having been taken, we pitched our tent in a muddy field that tens of thousands of sloshing feet and wheel-spinning vehicles had churned into a quagmire.

I turned my attention to the unparalleled opportunity to meet sexually liberated chicks—admittedly my main motivation for this venture. But the bevies of half-naked nubile flower children—subsequently so prominent in the news clips, the film of the festival, and my imagination—were nowhere to be seen. They undoubtedly occupied the prime spots. Partying couples, panhandlers, and mud-splattered stoners—lost in their own trips—offered limited opportunities for social intercourse and none of the more satisfying variety. Nevertheless, with three more festival days to go, I put on an optimistic front so as not to dampen my friends' enthusiasm: Wow! Look at all the people. Power to the people. All the power to all the people. Et cetera.

But nothing could stay dry in the sea of mud. After we'd spent several sleepless hours shivering in sodden sleeping bags, my high school best friend, Peter, suggested we skedaddle. Having someone to now blame for our wimping out, the rest of us concurred.

By then, my car had sunk so far into the muck that we had to dragoon ten stoned hippies to lug it back to the road.

On the drive back, we learned that we'd fled from history's greatest youth lovefest—a huge step up from the Slaying of the Firstborn, the Slaughter of the Innocents, and the Children's Crusade. This was my first experience of the reality of an event in which I'd been involved being profoundly different from the way it was portrayed in the media and conceived of by the public.

When I tell people I was there, they respond with awe tempered by jealousy. Knowing the importance of myth and legend to communal well-being, I don't disabuse them of their delusions. It's in their interest for them to think I was—and in an ineffable way still am—preternaturally hip.

One day, I'd have to confront the question of what I'd do after graduation. It wouldn't be an easy decision since I had no particular talent, and my ambition was largely directed at meeting girls. Given that difficulty, I wasn't about to ruin my senior year by worrying about my future. To the limited extent that I gave the matter any consideration, I thought I'd go to grad school in something or other—not out of intellectual interest, but rather to maintain my student draft deferral. Besides, although indifferent to the actual classes, I enjoyed the student lifestyle and sensed that, no matter what the future held, life would never be this carefree or magical again. There was however no immediate need to concern myself with the future; it wouldn't become a problem for another six months, and by then, something would come up.

Unfortunately, it did—earlier than expected.

VIII

Nix-on the Draft

December 1969–March 1970

Richard Milhous Nixon nixed the draft deferral for graduate students and instituted a lottery.

No reason to worry . . . yet. If I draw a high number, I'll be free. Free to do what? I'd decide some other time. But then . . .

On December 1, 1969, I pulled a 22 out of 365: a nonrefundable one-way third-class ticket to Saigon—unless I could find a loophole.

Looking for ways to beat the draft (I'd told myself that I had a moral objection to the war; but a bigger motivation might've been my desire to avoid death, maiming, or wasting my time doing unpleasant stuff), I asked a health service shrink to write a letter saying I was too crazy to napalm Vietnamese children in order to save them from Communism. He refused. But when I told him I wanted to cancel my therapy, he, overcome by separation anxiety, offered to prescribe me whatever pills I wanted if I'd continue. Much of the following sessions involved me counseling him on his insecurity issues, which essentially came down to an unfunny version of Rodney Dangerfield's tagline: "I got no respect." Although he wore a caduceus tie clip and had a med school diploma on the wall so patients wouldn't forget he was an MD, Larry Kasdan—my fraternity brother, close friend, and housemate—suggested he was an impostor who snuck into rooms and saw patients when the actual doctors weren't there.

Disappointed that I was insufficiently crazy, I asked another university doctor to examine my knees—a long shot, but worth trying if I didn't want to actually get shot. He measured the circumference of my thighs, explaining that he was testing for atrophy, a sign of torn cartilage, in those pre–CT scan days.

"Is that the standard test used by . . . oh, I don't know, the . . . um . . . well, the draft board, for example?" I asked.

"Yes. In fact, I do exams there once a week."

Yes!

His test turned up negative, so for the next three months, I did one-legged deep knee bends with a weight on my shoulders and used only my left leg to climb stairs—all with the goal of building up my left quadriceps to make it appear that, by comparison, I had atrophy of my right thigh. By the time of my draft physical, I'd created a noticeable difference of three-quarters of an inch between my thighs. But would it work?

At the draft physical, the white kids lined up in their underwear, carrying briefcases crammed with documentation of fanciful or exaggerated maladies. Fuck! The military men overseeing the physical had to be savvy enough to realize they and I were draft-dodging lollygaggers. In a vain attempt to improve my case, I put on a dramatic limp and walked hunched over like I was auditioning for the title role in *Richard III*, although no one seemed to notice and certainly no one cared. I was so scared I feared I'd vomit on the first official that spoke to me. *Would that help or hurt my case?*

The Black and Latino kids marched along, ready to do their duty, become addicted to Asian brown heroin, and frag their officers. Shame and nausea partially replaced my terror. When my country went to war, did I have an obligation to go even though I didn't believe in the cause? Was it wrong for me to sit back and let others fight and die in my place? I considered not mentioning my knee issue and doing my duty.

However, when it came time to see the doctor (luckily, not the one who'd examined me at the University of Michigan Health Service), I told him about my supposed malady. Then he got out his tape measure . . .

Success! I was 4-F, the "Selective Service classification designating a person considered physically, psychologically, or morally unfit for military duty." I was free! A huge weight came off my shoulders. As for my shame and nausea, the human capacity for self-righteousness and rationalization handled that—as long as I didn't dwell on it. As Ben Franklin said, "So convenient a thing to be a reasonable creature since it enables one to find or make a reason for everything one has a mind to do." To paraphrase Neil Armstrong, my draft ploy was a small limp forward for one childish man and a giant step for the unexamined life.

As I walked out of there, I had to lift my right leg with my hand in order to navigate the curb.

I later realized that Tricky Dick had made an unspoken deal with the middle class. If their kids clearly communicated that they *really* didn't want to go, then they didn't have to. In those days, white privilege, rather than the scourge it has become, was seen as the natural order of things. After all, God was white—formerly an Englishman, but now an American—and he had unlimited privilege.

For some, however, beating the draft took more effort than the others. While chopping off one's trigger finger was no longer fashionable, a Michigan acquaintance told the draft board examining psychologist that he'd kill himself if he was drafted. When the shrink pooh-poohed him, my schoolmate took a razor blade from the elastic band of his underwear and slit his wrist. They drafted him anyway but released him after his third suicide attempt. A friend of a friend overdosed on aspirin to give himself an ulcer—this after an attempt to starve himself to get under the required weight list had failed. Others fled to Canada.

My best friend from law school, Frank, had volunteered as he was planning a political career and didn't want to appear to be a draft evader. He ended up in Germany, writing for the American military newspaper, *Stars and Stripes*. However, listening to him describe his service, you'd have thought he was a second lieutenant in the paratroopers, whose life span in combat was eighteen minutes.

The war had been a mistake in that the United States had backed an unpopular, corrupt government. Also, like both sides in most wars, our soldiers committed atrocities. But in this war, their barbarity played out on TV. Like belching and nose-picking, atrocities are best committed out of public view; and when they aren't, it tends to harm the perpetrators' reputations. Once Nixon got rid of the draft in 1973, however, the protests stopped, moral objections notwithstanding. Too bad, as antiwar protests had been the ideal inexpensive date to make a positive impression on a woman with progressive[12] sensibilities or to meet women who were into exemplary liberal causes, such as sexual liberation and legalization of weed.

Beating the draft on my knees, so to speak, hadn't been a total scam. Four decades later, I had to have both my knees replaced.

---

[12] Now the only progressive things about me are the lenses of my glasses.

When I got out of the hospital, having had them both done at the same time, I didn't have a leg to stand on.

Beating the draft took a huge load off my shoulders, freeing me up to enjoy the last months of my college career or at least to obsess about the most pressing issues—sex, drugs, and rock 'n' roll.

Damn it all! At some point, I'd have to decide what to do after college as it was starting to appear that that issue also wouldn't resolve itself.

IX

I Star in the First Film by an Internationally Known Director

1969–1970

In my senior year at Michigan, the dorm system had published a "pig book," which featured pictures of the members of the freshman class. The most enticing entry had a passing resemblance to the Playmate of the Month whose photos had inspired me to apply to Michigan. She was a blonde dance student from the Chicago area with the intriguing name of Tiger. I impressed her with my phony radical sophistication—to paraphrase Mel Brooks, it was good to be a senior. Although we spent the night together several times a week, she was intent on saving her virginity for her high school boyfriend, so we pleased each other in other ways. Just the same, we enjoyed each other's company for several months. It wasn't a great romance as Tiger still fantasized about marrying her high school boyfriend. Also, since Sally had broken my heart, I was waiting for it to heal, hopefully without leaving excessive scar tissue.

In that same year, the late '60s zeitgeist took a toll on the fraternity system. My friend Sport, a compulsively friendly natural politician, got himself elected president of the fraternity and came up with the novel idea of making our frat coed. He reveled in the scathing press coverage from the *Detroit Free Press*, known on campus as the *Detroit Repress* for its conservative editorial policy—gosh, we were so clever. Reducing the issues to the most extreme satirical absurdity, the local right-wing media asked, "When will this insanity end? Coed bathrooms? Girls serving in combat units?"

A few months thereafter, one of our brothers made a huge heart on the floor of his room with hundreds of candles for Valentine's Day and then went to pick up his girlfriend. By the time he returned to the frat house, the entire place was ablaze, and coed fraternities ended up on the literal ash heap of history.

After presiding over the incineration of our frat house, Sport went to the University of Wisconsin Law School. After graduating, he stayed in Madison, where he founded a law firm with a notorious radical who was later elected mayor of the city. They organized their firm on socialist principles, meaning that the lawyers and secretaries shared equally in the firm's revenues. As a result, the secretaries made less than they would have if they'd had regular secretarial jobs. Sport went on to be elected as a trial judge, the second youngest in Wisconsin's history—a feat somewhat marred by the fact that Joe McCarthy, the infamous exploiter of the '50s Red Scare, had been the all-time youngest Wisconsin judge.

Disraeli described second marriages as "the triumph of hope over experience." What would he have said about Sport, who's now been married four times? Perhaps the triumph of magical thinking.

Sport recently shared with me photos of a sexy naked twentysomething Frenchwoman, with whom he'd struck up an email relationship and with whom he'd planned to travel around Europe as soon as the COVID pandemic ended.

"Don't send her money," I said.

"Thanks for the positive assumption."

"I see what's in it for you," I said. "But what's in it for her?"

"As a Jewish retired judge who rides a motorcycle, I'm intriguing."

"Oh, of course. The French are famous for their love of old Jews on wheels."

He's recently had a commitment ceremony—whatever that is—with a wonderful woman whose company he enjoys. He seems happy, posting multitudinous selfies on Facebook taken on their many vacations as well as photos of meals they've prepared. It seems they imagine that an admiring army of fanatical groupies has an unquenchable need to keep abreast of the minutiae of their daily lives. Perhaps they're influencers—whatever that is. Anyway, there are worse things than incurable optimism combined with social skills and genuinely liking people—not that I know from personal experience.

Having moved out of the frat house the year before the fire, I shared an off-campus house with my fraternity brothers Michael (my aforementioned LSD trip partner), Larry Kasdan, and two other guys. It was one of the most pleasant living experiences of my life.

With some legitimacy, Larry styled himself as the Sage from Morgantown, West Virginia. One of his observations, which I found useful, was that people aren't what they're like when they bare their souls in late-night heart-to-heart conversations. Rather, they are what their day-to-day actions show them to be.

Once, when I ran a red light with him in the car, he said, "I don't mind if I die, but I'd hate to be paralyzed for life from a traffic accident." From then on, I drove more carefully. At least I generally did, not counting the time when I drag-raced against my fraternity brother Mark Phillips on a two-lane road, with one of us starting out in the oncoming lane of traffic. I blew out my transmission in the process, but hey, I won.

Larry also talked me out of being photographed nude for a pornographic photography book and of dealing drugs even though I had a line on a hundred tabs of psilocybin at a bargain price. I'd like to think that I'd have come to the same conclusions without him, but much of what I'd like to think never comes to fruition.

I starred in Larry's first film, made for a campus festival in which the fraternities participated. Playing a fearsome gunslinger of the Old West, I aggressively shoved open the swinging doors of a saloon, only to be knocked down when they swung back.

While an acknowledged wise man, even if he was cursed with an annoying level of maturity, Larry was also a good listener and blessed with an engaging dry sense of humor. He laughed at my attempts at humor and acknowledged my occasional sagacious statement—when one talks as much as I did, some nuggets of wisdom are bound to emerge if only by the laws of probability. Little did I know that all that damn listening had an ulterior motive.

In Larry's breakout film, *The Big Chill*, the obnoxious character played by Jeff Goldblum recited various aperçus that I'd shared with Larry, such as "On some level, everyone does everything just to get laid" and "Don't knock rationalization. Where would we be without it? I don't know anyone who could get through the day without two or three juicy rationalizations. They're more important than sex." Hmm, now that writing this damn autobiography has forced me to think about my past (*examine*? God, I hope not), I realize I must've known about rationalizations well before I started practicing law—probably even while I was perpetrating high school election dirty tricks.

Rhetorical question: did Larry give me any credit for having crafted those and other lines?

Years later, he gave the University of Michigan commencement address, in which he said, "Your good friends from college may be the best friends you ever have. Guard those relationships like gold. Work hard to maintain them." The hypocrite has never attended any of our fraternity reunions; and when our mutual friends are in LA, he's too busy to see them, although when I was out there, he found time to meet me for breakfast. He does however keep up with the friends of his college girlfriend and later wife, MEG, an acronym for Mary Ellen Goldman. Disappointing, but no real surprise as most men tend to leave the planning of their social lives to their wives—a minor hardship for me as Amy is far less social than me.

No, *hypocrite* is too harsh or, rather, meaningless as we're all hypocrites in some way or another. It's just that I resent the loss of my former close friends; and it's easier to blame Larry, or rather MEG, than myself. Larry and I shared many laughs and enlightening conversations. He was brilliant, talented, and engaging; and while at our age it's hard to know, he probably still is. I wish I could still consider him a friend. Hey, Larry, wouldn't this autobiography make a great feature film?

It was deceptively easy to make friends at school, and it's turned out to be all too disappointingly easy to lose them. As time passed, many moved to other parts of the country, got married, had kids, and became caught up in family obligations, or, more recently, died or disappeared into the fog of dementia. The older I've gotten, the harder it's been to make new friends to replace those I've lost through attrition. I continue to try, however, and to make extra effort to hold on to those I had. I miss all my lost friends, some such as Larry more than others.

X

Cool like Kerouac

April 1970

Although I had only the vaguest idea of what lawyers actually did, I was a good talker and thought well on my feet. When I was growing up, *Perry Mason* and other TV lawyer shows made the practice of law look cool and kind of fun. In high school, to the limited extent I'd considered the subject of what I'd do for a living, I'd thought I'd go to business school and learn how to be an entrepreneur. In 1970, however, business was no longer in style; and being a lawyer could be spun in a way to make it appear hip. I could use my law degree to campaign for civil rights, help the poor, or . . . not that I had any such plans. Indeed, I had no idea what I'd do once I joined the bar. Law school was socially acceptable, and it meant that for the next three years, I wouldn't need to concern myself with the future.

I was caught up in the zeitgeist of the era but had no particular convictions. It wasn't only my unexamined life, but also I realized that most of the proponents of radical ideas were superficial poseurs. I thought of myself as superior because I recognized my superficiality, while they took themselves, and their fly-by-night convictions, so damn seriously. Sure, I wanted to make something significant of my life and to make a positive contribution to society.

But I had no idea how to make that happen and wasn't about to expend much effort to figure it out. I'd enjoyed living with friends in Ann Arbor and had a vague idea of maybe living communally in Vermont with a group of fascinating friends and practicing law. Had I given the future even a modicum of thought, I'd have realized that my frivolousness would lead to a disastrous comeuppance, which, as you'll soon see, it did. I, however, still had three more years of school to fritter away before my downfall would force me to grow the fuck up.

Anyway, I applied to law school. Writing this, I'm again struck by how little thought went into each of my life-changing decisions and how I was so stupidly concerned about impressing other people. I'd yet to realize that people were so wrapped up in worrying about what others thought of them that what I, or anyone else, did barely registered with them. What path would my life have taken if I'd more carefully researched and thought out my alternatives and paid less mind to what impression I'd be making on others? I'd probably have screwed up my life much more thoughtfully and creatively than I did.

In spite of my frivolity and commitment to the unexamined life, I always got good grades—one of the reasons that my parents were so unconcerned about what I did. Michigan, Columbia, and NYU law schools accepted me. Berkeley and Stanford wait-listed me, so naturally, they became my first choices—sort of like how Sally made herself the love of my college years by keeping me on her emotional waiting list. As the epicenter of the revolution, California was cool— perfect for me as I was cool, hip, and groovy. Since I'd surely have to choose between the two schools (it was imaginable that they'd turn me down given that I'd gone to the effort of applying and was so damn charming), I had to visit. I got a ride as far as Boulder, Colorado, from Michael—my frat brother, college housemate, LSD trip mate, and Woodstock venture companion. I hitchhiked the rest of the way west, and a well-worn copy of *On the Road* jammed into my back pocket so the title would stick out.

Not that Kerouac's spontaneous prose style appealed to me. Indeed, I agreed with what Truman Capote famously said about the book: "That isn't writing; it's typing." Still, what else would an ostentatiously, but superficially hip hitchhiker be reading? I'd considered, but rejected, *The Hitchhiker's Guide to the Universe*. Although I loved the book, I feared it wouldn't be the ideal prop as it would betray a lack of serious commitment to the nitty-gritty of hitching. Sure, I knew that almost no one would notice and no one at all would care what I was reading. Yet when trying to project a certain image, it's crucial to get the minor details right. If I could make myself believe I appeared to be hip and cool, perhaps I could convince others—not that anyone gave a flying fuck.[13]

A lapsed Mormon picked me up on the Interstate 80 entrance ramp. After chugging a can of beer every twenty miles or so, he— voice choked with tears—invited me to accompany him on a detour to visit his parents' graves, which I turned down, hoping for an upgrade to a sober driver.

After three hot, dusty hours standing by the side of the road regretting that decision, a pickup truck with an "America: Love It or Leave It" bumper sticker and gun rack stopped for me. I jumped in.

I could've done without the cowboy hat–wearing driver's harangues about how the hippies should have the courage of their convictions and pour gasoline over themselves and set themselves

---

[13] I recently learned that that expression didn't refer to doing it on an airplane but rather copulating while bouncing along on horseback, which seems to me to present something of a challenge. But then again, I thought I was being kinky if I screwed on a chair, floor, or beach.

aflame like the Buddhist fucking monks, his heartfelt regrets over not having killed more gooks when he was in Nam, and his outrage over the national disgrace that Lieutenant Calley was prosecuted for bullshit war crimes rather than being awarded a medal for his service at My Lai. On the bright side, he cruised along at thirty above the limit. I figured that the faster he drove, the shorter the time I'd be exposed to danger. When we reached the bleak heart of the desert, an ominous silence descended upon us.

Eyes no longer on the road, he scanned the barren landscape. He suddenly swerved onto a side road, then careened down a bumpy unmarked dirt track. When out of sight of the highway, he slammed on the brakes, popped the glove compartment, and withdrew a *six-gun*! All without a word. I was scared silent, not that suggesting that he refrain from killing me would've made a difference. Presumably, he could intuit my position on the subject. He raised his gun and . . .

Shot a rabbit, tossed the carcass onto the cargo bed, returned to the truck, and drove on. Shortly thereafter, having reached his exit, he dropped me off on the interstate in an area so devoid of signs of human habitation that its highest and best use would've been as an H-bomb test site.

The few cars on the road sped by. I slouched against a signpost in the Nevada desert covered with a seven-foot-long ode to hitchhikers' despair and graffiti such as "Been here 4 days 6 hours nothing." Although warm during the day, the high-desert March night fell hard and cold—not normal cold, but a potentially killing cold.

The next morning, unable to feel my fingers or toes and teeth aching from a night of chattering, an elderly woman stopped for me. Her wheezing ancient Volkswagen Bug lacked a working heater, but the day warmed as we went. She drove me all the way to Palo Alto while entertaining me with tales of the four scumbags she'd married.

Curiously, each of them had died under what seemed to me to be increasingly suspicious circumstances—the penultimate one eating poisonous mushrooms and the last one taking a fatal fall down a flight of stairs. Maybe he'd refused to eat the mushrooms—not a problem as I, although appreciative of the ride, didn't intend to marry her or share a mushroom omelet.

On arriving in the Bay Area, I learned that both schools had rejected me. Their letters implied that I'd have been a shoo-in in prior years, but that year, they'd had a record number of applications. Evidently, I hadn't been the only one who'd thought it'd be cool to attend law school in California.

So fine, I went to Columbia, where my obsession with trying to appear cool and somehow larger-than-life fully blossomed.

XI

Like Raquel Welch Playing USO Gigs in a String Bikini

March 1971

Professor Berger taught Property Law, a required course for first-year Columbia Law School students. Rather than sit on the chair provided or stand at the lectern, Berger perched precariously on a divider between the teachers' area and the students' seats, his pants riding up to display his hip white socks. Never mind that they hadn't been hip for a decade. He was a change of pace from the fuddy-duddy old teachers who sat behind a desk or stood at a podium. Comfortable with their superiority, they felt no need to pretend to be friends with their students; and as mature adults, the fads and lunacies of the early '70s didn't affect them. I preferred the more traditional professors, but no one asked for my opinion.

"I'm very distressed," he began, as if we cared about his mental state. We only wanted to know what would be on the exam. The more serious students also wanted to hear about property law, but they were as indifferent to his distress as he was to theirs. "I read in the paper that many of you young people don't intend to participate in the upcoming march on Washington to protest the Vietnam War. So we're going to devote the entire class to discussing this plague of apathy."

"I woke up before noon for this?" I said to my friend Brewie. "The guy spends his working life on a university campus and has to read the *Times* to ascertain what students think."

He nodded his agreement, then rested his head in his hands.

Meanwhile, a solid 40 percent of the class jumped at the brownnosing opportunity and feigned concern over Berger's purported or rhetorical *distress*. I had my own reasons for being distressed—my sex life. But unlike him, I didn't have the emotional release of porking a married first-year law student.

Former political science majors intent on telling Berger what he wanted to hear said things like "The only way to bring about change is to press the various governmental pressure points. A protest march garners media attention, which in turn pressures . . . Blah blah blah." Maybe they hadn't actually said *blah blah blah*, but it wasn't easy to hear over Brewie's snoring in the seat next to mine.

Someone in the horde of indistinguishable suck-ups—maybe my friend Jack (more about him later)—aping Berger's melancholy tone, said, "I've gone on several marches and always come back frustrated. The war goes on. People die. Nothing changes."

Not satisfied with having wasted half the class, Berger began calling on us backbenchers.

"Mr. Mouse," he said. Getting no response, he raised his voice. "Mickey Mouse."

We'd had to fill out seating charts at the beginning of the semester. Never missing an opportunity to be total assholes, Brewie and I had signed in as Disney characters.

"Mr. Duck," he said to me, only realizing his mistake when the class broke into laughter.

One of the front-row strivers had clued him into our names.

"Mr. Brewster," he said, raising his voice, again getting no response.

"Mr. Chan, wake up Mr. Brewster."

"You put him to sleep," I said quite reasonably. "You wake him up."

Class participation didn't count. Having learned in first semester how to fill blue books with exemplary blather (the key to law school exams is to cite all possible issues that arise from a certain hypothetical), I believed I'd ace the anonymously submitted exam. So I had no reason to play his game. Indeed, I could barely play my own game.

The shocked, nervous laughter of my classmates caused Brewie to stir. A descendant of Elder Brewster, not just a mere passenger, but the chaplain on the *Mayflower*, Brewie was not about to interrupt his sleep to please a parvenu poseur.

"You've yet to speak on this issue, Mr. Chan," Professor Berger said. "You must have an opinion."

Well, if I must.

"Well, shit," I began, getting everyone's attention. Even Brewie woke up. "I've gone on a whole bunch of marches and *never* came back frustrated. Spring comes early in Washington—cherry blossoms, scantily dressed teenyboppers, and all that.

"On the drive down, you liberate all the candy by the checkout counters at the roadside Howard Johnson's. In DC, you swim naked in the reflecting pool between the Lincoln Memorial and the Washington Monument. Just be sure to stay far enough from the antiwar speeches so they're reduced to unintrusive background noise. Get high with hippie chicks and barely legal runaways in various stages of nakedness. Write *fuck* on your forehead, score some shrooms, and spout silly slogans like 'Drop pants, not bombs,' 'Johnson pull out like your father should've,' 'Freedom means the right to shout *theater* in a crowded fire,' and 'One, two, three, four, end the war. Five, six, seven, eight, free Huey. Smash the state.'

"If you want to bring people around to your cause, make it fun. And if that fails, so what? At least you've had a great time."

Stunned silence. Heads turned sideways, almost as far as that of the possessed girl in *The Exorcist*. Then as if on time delay, there was sustained enthusiastic laughter and applause. Starved for sensory input, law students were an easy audience. It was like being Raquel Welch playing USO gigs in a thong-string bikini.

In a frenzied effort to be called on in the limited time remaining, the strivers raised their hands as high as they could. No telling how many first-year law students tore their rotator cuffs trying to get Berger's attention.

When they were called on, they said things like "I agree with Chan. The only way to bring about change is to put pressure on the various governmental pressure points, and a protest march garners useful media attention. Blah blah blah." Maybe they hadn't actually said *blah blah blah*, but it wasn't easy to hear as Brewie had resumed his snoring.

That speech marked the high point of my compulsive effort to appear to be larger-than-life, although it took many years and much emotional battering for my conduct to approach the acceptable range of normal. Decades later, I had a girlfriend who, after we'd been dating for several months, said of my dogged athletic pursuits, "Do you realize that you're overcompensating for being short?"

I dumped her immediately, appalled that she'd been so unobservant as to have failed to notice that on our first date.

Before going to law school, I equated intelligence with seeing the world the way I did. In law school, though, I realized that many of my classmates were extremely bright, even though their worldviews were quite different from my own.

Many of them were more mature than me because they'd served in the military or otherwise taken time off between college and law school. Another explanation is that they were serious, ambitious people who'd gone to law school as a first step toward being successful lawyers. Unlike me, they knew what the practice of law actually involved and knew that was what they wanted to do. In short, law school offered me a glimpse of the real world. Too bad my eyes were blinkered.

Initially, I'd been lonely in law school, missing the comfortable life and the many friends I'd had in Ann Arbor.[14] Ultimately, though, I made lifelong friends in law school, such as Brewie, who is a frequent dinner and theater companion to this day. When I started my own law firm, several of them turned out to be significant sources of business, such as the trademark licensing agent I will mention later. Perhaps because I went to law school in New York and many of the graduates remained there, I have more friends from law school than high school or college.

---

[14] Three of my frat brothers—my housemate and Woodstock companion, Michael, and my drag racing companions, Joe and Mark—remained in Ann Arbor, where they founded a string of stereo stores that became the model for the running shoe stores in Larry Kasdan's *The Big Chill*. For some time, particularly after their company went public, I regretted not having joined them.

Decades later, my son, Adam, went to Columbia Law School and took it far more seriously than I had. Consequently, he enjoyed the educational experience and got far more out of it than I had. I'd gone to law school to get a degree, with the vague hope that I'd figure out something rewarding to do with it. But if I had the chance to do it over again . . . Doesn't matter as life doesn't give us mulligans. So let's leave it at I'm proud of my son, but also a bit envious.

XII

Tiger! Tiger! Burning Bright

April 1971

When I was in my first semester in law school, Tiger dropped out of Michigan and showed up in New York unannounced to try to make it as a dancer. I took her to a poetry reading party given by my pretentious previously mentioned law school friend Jack, then back to my place. We started necking. But then, well after midnight, she insisted on going back to the crime-ridden depths of Brooklyn, where she was staying with a friend.

Although annoyed as there was no legitimate reason why she couldn't have stayed over, I played the unaccustomed role of the gentleman and accompanied her on an hour-and-a-half subway journey, which included three line changes, adding to my annoyance. On my return trip on the electric sewer, I met a hippie chick wearing a dozen multicolored scarves and little else. When Jack asked if it would be okay if he took Tiger out, I told him it was. After all, she couldn't have made it any clearer she wasn't interested in a sexual relationship with me.

A year later, when it was way too late for me to do anything about it, he told me that, when they were together, she'd call out my name in her sleep. According to him, she'd come to New York primarily to get it on with me and only secondarily to make it as a dancer. She'd told Jack that she hadn't slept with me that night because she'd wanted to wait until everything was perfect—not that she'd given me any indication of that or that Jack had told me when I'd have had a chance to do something about it. I don't know if things could've worked between us, but I'd have liked to have given it a try.

My life would have been so much better if women realized that, like many men, I don't pick up on subtlety and that if they wanted something from me, they had to express their desires clearly and straightforwardly as if speaking to a dim-witted child. In most cases, I'd have been delighted to do what they wanted, if only I knew what that was. Women often joke about, or bitch about, how slow men are to pick up on their hints. So realizing that, why don't they give us a break and be straightforward with us? Even the most seemingly mindless females suddenly transform into geniuses when the conversation turns to the nuances or subtle aspects of relationships.

In any event, after several months with Jack, Tiger returned to Michigan and married a Detroit accountant. Even though I never met the guy, I have no doubt that as, boring as he likely was, he was a step up from Jack.

After my "write *fuck* on your forehead" speech, Jack said, "I can't tell if you're brilliant or crazy."

"They're not mutually exclusive," I replied.

When the law firm he went to work for out of law school fired him, Jack wheedled himself into the position of general counsel for the state agency tasked with building the Javits Convention Center. About a year later, that agency came to its collective senses and canned him. They were so delighted to see the back of him that they gave him a celebratory going-away party. Panicked that no one would show up,[15] he invited me to attend. "You'll get an opportunity to meet Kevin, the new general counsel, who could be a huge source of legal business for you," he said, deaf to the irony; during his stint on the job, he'd failed to refer a cent of business to me. Having the uncanny ability to land better jobs each time he was fired, he retired rich to Sun Valley after a commercial bank bought out the investment bank he was working for and paid him a substantial sum just to get rid of him.

I'm not sure why I'm being so critical of Jack. He had his foibles, which I enjoyed pointing out. But all in all, he wasn't a bad guy. I suppose I resent that in spite of my efforts to keep up with him, he didn't reciprocate after he'd stumbled into relative riches. When he periodically came to New York City, flying his private plane into New Jersey's Teterboro Airport, he never bothered to call.

By the way, Jack introduced me to a woman; and after a pleasant, but mutually unsatisfactory date, I fixed her up with Brewie. Nearly four decades later, they are still happily married, with a recently married daughter.

At a Columbia party, in my second year of law school, a law school friend bemoaned that as short guys, we didn't stand a chance with desirable women. To prove him wrong, I approached the most attractive one in the room. She accompanied me to my penthouse apartment, a converted maid's quarters on the roof of a building on Cathedral Parkway (110th Street), for $130 per month including all

---

[15] He needn't have been concerned. His going-away party was like the funeral of the universally hated Harry Cohn, a cofounder and president of Columbia Pictures Corporation. When all of Hollywood turned out for it, Red Skelton explained, "Give the public what they want, and they'll come out for it."

utilities. We got high and started necking. I came immediately and after that remained flaccid. Lying on top of her, I kept thinking, *I don't know what to say*. But instead of just thinking it, I was saying it out loud. The experience shook me deeply and left me impotent or, more accurately, afraid of coming prematurely or otherwise failing to perform, which amounted to the same thing.

The summer after my first year in law school, I had a job as a hip, radical young legal assistant for Vermont Legal Aid, where I finally got a peek at what it was like to practice law and thought I might like it. I enjoyed hiking the Green Mountains on weekends and the camaraderie of a tight-knit legal community devoted to doing good. Most importantly, I hooked up with a woman who eased me inside her before I realized what was happening, and everything worked fine. Great, actually. I was cured!

A few weeks later, she compared Kissinger and Nixon unfavorably to Hitler. I pointed out that Vietnam wasn't quite the Holocaust, and she replied, "You Jews are all the same—never thinking of anyone but yourselves."

I dressed and left without another word. Anti-Semitism turns up in the most unexpected places. Also, of course, in the most expected places.

When I returned to New York from my Vermont summer job, my sex life went into high gear and, by some measure, peaked, even if my primary relationship ended in tragedy. But more about that later.

XIII

Get Out of Town before Sundown

December 1971

First semester of the second year at Columbia Law School, classes ended in mid-December with finals the first week of January. Merry Christmas, happy fucking New Year.

After reading a note on a Columbia University message board, looking for someone to share the expense of driving to Aspen for a week of skiing, I deluded myself into believing that I knew the material and that overstudying could be deleterious to my grade point average.

When we reached Nebraska and I took my shift at the wheel, we hit an ice storm; or rather, it hit us. A white-knuckle hour later, I swerved to avoid a jackknifed semi, sending the car into a series of 360-degree spins.

"Please pull over when you can," my companion, a scraggly-haired philosophy grad student, said upon waking up from a fitful sleep.

He got out, vomited, and returned to the passenger seat. I continued driving.

Arriving in Aspen without further incident, I stopped in one of the few downscale restaurants for a slice of pizza and a line on an inexpensive room. Before I could order, the pizza chef quit. The owner had directed him to use pre-frozen pizza dough. He refused as a matter of principle, declaring that that would be like using Cheez Whiz in fondue. I bought him a beer, and he invited me to sleep on the floor of a house he shared with several other ski bums.

Three days later, on my return from skiing, two Pitkin County sheriff's deputies—complete with ten-gallon hats, five-pointed stars, and large holstered six-guns—were waiting to question me in connection with a drugstore robbery. I told them I didn't know anything about it. But when one of them shot me a hostile stare while easing his gun out of its holster, I, as a good citizen, agreed to accompany them to the police station.

The bad cop, or rather the worse cop, read me my Miranda rights. Having only recently read *Miranda v. Arizona* in Criminal Procedure, I smiled. The primary rule we'd learned in class was *never waive your rights and always request a lawyer*. Suspects often waive their rights, thinking it will make a good impression and make them appear to be innocent, but that only gets the cops' blood up. NEVER DO THAT! The police aren't your friends.

"I don't need a lawyer," I said. "I have nothing to hide."

I knew that had been a mistake as soon as the words left my mouth. Having done nothing wrong, however, I wanted to get this over with quickly. I just wanted to take off my sweaty ski clothes, take a shower, have a beer, and study for exams. The rationale that I knew the material and overstudying could be deleterious to my grade point average had evaporated when, soon after my arrival, I began reviewing my Civil Procedure notes and found them to be an infelicitous combination of the illegible and the incoherent.

The deputy sheriff's smile made me remember reading that when chimpanzees, the species most biologically similar to us, bare their teeth, it's a sign of aggression.

I explained that I was just crashing on the floor and if the loot had been hidden under the bed or somewhere, I wouldn't have seen or known about it.

He leaned forward, put his right hand on his gun butt, and, in a tone so accusatory it must've been copied from TV police procedurals, asked, "How did you know the stolen property was under the bed?"

"Unlucky guess. It was a small room." I wiped a droplet of sweat from my forehead. "Not many places to stash something."

After an incredulous, tight-lipped nod, he said, "I don't suppose you have an alibi for last night between ten and midnight?"

"As a matter of fact, I do. I was with a woman in Snowmass."

"This so-called woman have a name?"

I gave him her name and number. But then, with an awful sinking feeling, I realized that if she, as a small-time weed dealer, got a call from the police, she'd deny knowing me, if only for my own protection. The police, known then as the *pigs*, were the enemy in those days, as we were to them. (Trump didn't invent tribalism or polarization. My generation did—one of our few lasting accomplishments.)

"Would you be willing to take a lie detector test, you know, just so we can rule you out?" the less bad cop asked.

"Sure." I shrugged my shoulders. That effort to appear casual would've been more convincing had my shoulders not been too tense to properly shrug. "Hook me up."

"The polygraph machine is up in Loveland County. No one will be available to operate it until after New Year's, but you'll be fine here in jail."

"I can't do that. I need to be back in New York next week for final exams." Also, a felony conviction would have strangled my legal career in its cradle. Even an arrest would have to be disclosed on my application to the bar. Determining when a custodial interrogation morphs into a formal arrest can be a tricky legal question. So at that point, I could still have truthfully said that I hadn't been arrested since I hadn't been booked or fingerprinted even though I'd been in custody. Although I hadn't tested the proposition, I probably wasn't free to leave. A week spent in jail, however, would surely constitute an arrest and would have had to be disclosed.

He laughed so hard I thought he'd swallowed a hair ball. More to the point, I feared his gun would go off accidentally and blow his foot off or, rather, mine.

"I want a lawyer," I said.

After leaving me to stew for a while, he returned with the Yellow Pages. I perused the listing for lawyers, then called the only one listed with a Jewish name and explained my situation to him.

"Come on, kid. It's Christmas Eve. I doubt you'll be able to find anyone to help until after New Year's."

I spent the next several hours—each one feeling as if it had lasted for a day and a half—sitting in the empty interrogation room in my sweaty, clammy clothes and uncomfortable ski boots. All the while, I contemplated the death of my legal career and hoped that the stories of short white guys being raped in prison were exaggerated.

Finally, the sheriff came in.

"You're free to go. Your alibi checked out." Then he actually said, "But if I were you, I'd get out of town before sundown."

I returned to New York in time to ace all but one of my finals. I still don't understand why I got that B in Criminal Procedure.

But friends were impressed that I'd had balls—a euphemism for *stupidity* in this and most cases—to take off during finals study week. So what if that B meant I just missed being in the top 10 percent of my class? An A in Criminal Procedure wouldn't have gotten me laid any more than the B did, which was not at all.

XIV

Connoisseurship

June 1972

Kenny, the first of my high school friends to get married, invited me to his wedding to the daughter of a Jewish doctor from Rochester, New York.

Among the good times he and I had had in high school was the time he snuck up behind me in the library and, for no reason beyond his desire to demonstrate our friendship, sucker-punched me in the solar plexus, leaving me doubled up and gasping for air. Another memory, when we were both home on summer vacation from college, we made psychedelic light boxes (referred to in chapter II supra) out of indirect lighting plastic, blinking Christmas tree lights, and lumber that we'd liberated from a nearby construction site. Masquerading as hippie craftspeople, we peddled the light boxes to East Village head shops.

In any event, I arrived in time to attend the wedding rehearsal dinner, which was given by another doctor, a close friend of the bride's father who was renowned as an oenophile in the tight group of Jewish Rochester MDs. While somewhat motivated by affection for the bride and her family, his primary interest was showing off his wine cellar and his preeminent connoisseurship.

Carafes of decanted wine already displayed on the massive dining room table, our host bid us sit, and he began his spiel. "I envy you all. You're about to savor wines that are simply too special for laymen to ever get to imbibe. The first selection, 1959 Château Haut-Brion, is generally acknowledged to be one of the finest bottles ever corked."

After pouring a couple of ounces into his oversized crystal glass, he explained to us benighted neophytes that large glasses allowed the red wine to come into contact with more air and *breathe* more thoroughly.

As if choreographed, we all leaned forward with anticipation. Unbeknownst to him but known to all of us, his wife, as a joke to lighten the mood, had substituted cheap Gallo wine for the legendary tipple.

Slowly, dramatically, he brought his glass to his nose and took a deep sniff.

We waited for him to curl his lip in disgust. After we'd all have a good-natured laugh, the real stuff would be brought out for us to properly savor.

"Magnificent!" he exclaimed, pride and self-esteem emanating from his every pore.

We shifted uncomfortably in our seats but weren't deeply concerned as he had yet to taste the cheap plonk. We waited for his mouth to twist in disgust, then for him to spit it out.

He took a sip and . . . a smile of sublime satisfaction spread across his face.

"Even better than I remembered."

In this tight social group of doctors, where everyone knew one another and gossip was the mother's milk of conversation, he was publicly unmasked as a buffoon. None of his fellow doctors could ever tell him, but they couldn't restrain themselves from telling others. Soon, everyone had heard and enjoyed the story.

That dinner cemented my opinion of connoisseurship as pretentious bullshit.

I've devised a foolproof theorem for rating wine: divide the price by the alcohol content and order the wine with the lowest quotient.

Kenny became a gifted physician, and he's given me more articulate and useful medical advice than I received from most of the doctors I've had to pay for and for whom I've had to wait in their aptly named waiting rooms for hundreds of cumulative hours.[16] If this were his autobiography, he'd probably falsely claim to have invented the psychedelic light boxes, but then you'd have to wade through all sorts of boring crap about his medical career and all the grateful and worshipping people he'd cured.

In 1980, Kenny (now Ken) told me about a study that concluded that for ideal cardiovascular health, people should, at least three times a week, do exercise that gets their heartbeat up to 80 percent of the maximum beats per minute for at least twenty minutes. Over the ensuing four decades plus, I never did less than that, except when recuperating from one of my several orthopedic surgeries (described below).

Ken and I lost touch after we each got divorced, but we rekindled our friendship at our forty-fifth high school reunion. We spoke regularly during COVID; and those conversations, as well as those with other out-of-town friends, helped to keep me from going crazy or, rather, even crazier.

---

[16] On the subject of superior alternatives to medical examinations, a friend told me he went to a prostitute who, in the course of his session, stuck a finger up his butt to enhance his erotic pleasure. Afterward, she told him that his prostate was enlarged and spongy and advised him to seek treatment. He did, and according to him, it saved his life.

XV

Ann

Winter/Spring 1973

On the rare occasions that Ann deigned to take time off from her full-time paralegal job and show up for class at law school, she wore miniskirts, tight tops, and high heels.

A tall, thin dark-haired beauty with flawless alabaster skin, she was an advertisement for sex, even though that is the one product that needs no advertising.

Like the star of a '40s movie, she seemed more brightly lit than the rest of us. Being a genius, she could get away with treating law school as a minor inconvenience. Too bad she was married, not that I'd have had a chance with her even if she were single. But in *The Many Loves of Dobie Gillis*, the TV show I'd been watching when Peter called to tell me he'd smoked marijuana, the school principal had told the ne'er-do-well beatnik Maynard G. Krebs, "Your reach should exceed your grasp." On occasions, I'd followed that advice with decidedly mixed results. Passively hoping for a miracle did me no harm and, of course, little good.

Ann and I had never even spoken, and I had no reason to believe she even knew who I was. On one of her rare appearances at school, she, totally out of the blue, introduced herself and invited me over for dinner, telling me she'd been impressed by my "write *fuck* on your forehead" speech. As I didn't know any practicing lawyers, I looked forward to meeting her husband. In order to convey the impression that, although I sometimes played the part of the iconoclastic hippie manqué, I was the well-mannered boy that I actually was, I arrived with a bottle of wine and flowers. It was then that I learned she and her husband had separated. To celebrate, we stayed up all night. In the short breaks between our repeated lovemaking, she told me her extraordinary life story.[17]

She'd grown up in an ultra-Orthodox Jewish community in Brooklyn. Every man in her family, practically going all the way back to the destruction of the Second Temple, had been not merely a rabbi but also a famous one. To state the obvious, every woman had married one. Her father devoted his life to the study of the Torah, which required her mother to work at a dreary job to support the family in addition to raising their eight children—*only* eight children according to the community's pitying judgment. Ann's social life consisted of meetings in the living room with promising rabbinical students while her mother listened from the next room. Afterward, her mom asked Ann what she thought about the boy's husband potential. To the consternation of her parents, Ann not only failed to show interest in any of her arranged dates. But perhaps even worse, she also enrolled in college, where, contrary to God's law, males and females attended the same classes and freely socialized with each other.

After graduating summa cum laude from Brooklyn College in two and a half years, she became a teacher in one of Brooklyn's most violence-plagued slum high schools in order to pay the city back for

---

[17] Fictionalized in my novel *girl*, which I unreservedly and objectively recommend. See https://www.amazon.com/girl-Robert-N-Chan/dp/1630663816.

the free education it had given her. There, a Black janitor raped her in a school stairwell. Following a logic of her own, she began dating him. When people in her community saw the two of them together (particularly if they glimpsed the couple sinfully holding hands in public), they assumed the worst and didn't keep those assumptions to themselves. As a result, she was cast out by the tight-knit community, effectively excommunicating her from her family and everyone with whom she'd grown up. With nowhere else to live, she moved in with her rapist, a Black Panther, who slept with her with a loaded .357 Magnum pistol by his side. He taught her the joy of anal sex and the not-so-fine line between pain and pleasure.

When he went to prison for an armed robbery whose goal was to raise money for the Panthers, she met a Columbia Law School student at a party who took her back to his place. Not only did he turn out to be impotent, but also he soon came down with hepatitis. She nursed him through both maladies and approaching her life-altering decisions with an even more lackadaisical attention to detail and lack of concern than I'd devoted to such matters, she married him. While working full-time to support him, she wrote all his law school papers, earning him his only As. Seeing how easy law school was, she enrolled in Columbia.

Since she had to leave the marital abode, she moved in with me the day after our first night together. Abrupt? Yes, but our lovemaking that night had been persuasive.

As a challenge, when we lived together, I'd occasionally try to devise a way to touch her in bed so as not to make her come. I never succeeded. To the extent I had a *type*, I was most aroused by women who, by their enthusiastic responses to my ministrations, made me believe I was a great lover. That belief was self-fulfilling, creating an unvirtuous circle. I'd always been happy to suspend disbelief and believe a compliment, a well-faked orgasm, or, even better, multiple feigned orgasms. I told myself that given the huge variety of sexual tastes, it was possible that there existed a coterie of highly desirable women who were passionately aroused by short bald Jewish guys who believed they had a great sense of humor. If not in this universe, then maybe in another; all I needed to do was figure out how to get there. Ann, however, never needed to fake anything; and by a miraculous stroke of luck or perhaps a fortuitous alignment of the stars, she existed in the universe I inhabited.

The flip side of her extraordinary sexual responsiveness was a borderline-psychotic intensity. We'd have friends over for dinner; and if I'd go to the bathroom, she'd come in for a quickie, which made our friends and me uncomfortable. Like any couple, we'd fight occasionally. Unlike them, when we did, she'd hit me—hard—on the theory that words could wound more than fists. I'd lie face down on our bed while she pounded on my back until her anger was spent. Her eyes were two different colors: her jade-green eye frequently seemed to glow with pleasure, excitement, and erotic desire, while her light-brown eye, when half closed, presaged trouble.

Once, when driving back from a romantic weekend in a Vermont country inn, we got into an argument over something I considered inconsequential. She, though, apparently didn't as she threatened to turn the car into the oncoming lane of traffic if I didn't take her complaint more seriously. I had no doubt that she'd do it. Her craziness was as authentic as her multiple orgasms.

"Ann, you need to learn to dial it back," I told her on more than one occasion. "You're far too intense."

"I'm not like other people. I might die tomorrow."

"Please, don't be dramatic. Each of us might die tomorrow. As my father used to say, 'People are dying these days who never died before.'"

While I enjoyed her company when she wasn't acting out, which was most of the time, her crazy fits gnawed away at me, as did her alienation of my friends, who had the sense that she was about to come on to them even though she was totally faithful to me. Back then, I'd placed an inordinate importance on my male friendships. It would be ten years, a divorce, and abandonment by my best friend from law school (described below), before I realized the accuracy of Fitzgerald's axiom "It is in the thirties that we want friends. In the forties, we know they won't save us any more than love did." Being precocious, I beat his schedule by a decade.

Between my graduation from law school in May and the July bar exam, I, like almost all my classmates, took a bar review course. Such a course was necessitated because Columbia and the other self-characterized *national* law schools, unlike the lower-ranked local schools, didn't teach New York law, which was the subject of the New York bar exam. They prided themselves on instructing their students how to *think like* a lawyer—being able to see all sides of a problem, among other things, such as glib moral relativity. Should their graduates have a reason in their practice to know the actual law, they could research the issue and bill handsomely for their time doing so or hire a graduate from one of the lesser schools to do their scut work. Studying for the bar exam was a grueling, anxiety-ridden time. Unlike the local schools, which had a passing rate of well over 90 percent, Columbia's passing rate—like that of Yale, Harvard, etc.—hovered around 60 percent.

It wasn't sufficient to be smart. The entire body of New York law had to be memorized, and that took time and grinding effort. So

I studied as hard as I was able to and spent much of the rest of the time worrying that I wasn't studying sufficiently. Ann, though, didn't take a course; and being genius, she saw no reason to study—and plenty of reason to distract me. As I became increasingly uptight, her sexual voracity and desire to play rose to meet the challenge. Finally, her intensity became too much for me. After giving the matter uncharacteristic consideration, I asked her to move out.

Several weeks later, while I was in the midst of reconsidering my decision, I learned secondhand that she was found unconscious, phone off the hook, an empty bottle of pills by her side. She died in the hospital.

Showing up at my apartment out of the blue, having learned about me from her sexually explicit diary, one of her several brothers told me the hospital had tested her for a variety of drug overdoses and found nothing. In the meantime, she died of a diabetic coma. Although neither of us had known she was a diabetic, the hospital, according to him, had committed malpractice by failing to test for diabetes. That didn't make much sense. But as I've learned, it's often impossible to know the truth, and the senseless is often what's true. That might be one of the appeals of fiction as all the facts the author feels we need to know are set out right there, and any ambiguity is intentional.

When the bar exam results came out, I saw that she'd passed. I also did, but several of my more serious student friends hadn't.

Too late, I realized I'd been quite fond of her—maybe more than quite fond. I think of her often and wonder whether, if we'd stayed together, I could have saved her life. I should have been more tolerant of her angry flare-ups and instead concentrated on all the great things about her. If we'd gotten married and she hadn't died, we'd probably ultimately have gotten divorced. Most people do.

But we'd have had beautiful, brilliant kids; and by now, I'd have grandchildren. In these lonely times, I wish I had grandchildren and am jealous of my friends who get so much pleasure from theirs. *If* is the nastiest short word in our language, followed closely by *wish*.

After Ann and law school, I suffered through a seven-year downturn. Was it karma for my breaking up with Ann or for not having taken law school seriously, even if I did graduate in the top quarter of my class, albeit the bottom of that quarter? No, I got what I deserved and can't blame supernatural factors. It took me the biblical seven lean years to grow the fuck up and shake off my extended adolescent fascination with the counterculture and my juvenile efforts to appear hip and cool to people who couldn't have cared less.

And the rest is history—that is, tragic and farcical.

XVI

Two Impostors

1973–1980

After graduating law school, I moved to an apartment in a brownstone on Eighty-Second Street between West End Avenue and Riverside Drive, paying the princely rent of $325 per month. The phone company assigned me a new telephone number. My phone rang multiple times a day. The callers were a seemingly endless parade of alluring-voiced young women. They, however, weren't calling for me. They were for someone named Mike, the previous holder of the number. Finally, I asked one of them what was it about this guy that inspired such female loyalty long after he'd abandoned his phone number. After a thoughtful pause, she said, "Well, they used to call him Iron Mike." I considered initiating a legal proceeding to change my name to Iron Bob but ultimately realized it wouldn't help.

In accordance with my commitment to the unexamined life, I didn't investigate my employment prospects before making the major life decision of where to work after law school. I accepted an offer from a firm that touted itself as the fastest-growing firm in the city because its rapid growth promised unparalleled opportunities for advancement. As soon as I started to work there, however, it stopped growing, stopped making partners, and stopped training young associates. The firm, however, continued its culture of abuse, which I'd been unaware of when I accepted their offer.[18]

If judged by its bathrooms, the firm had three genders: men, women, and partners.[19] At the firm Christmas party, the receptionist performed a sexy belly dance wearing a gossamer harem girl costume, and one of the senior partners porked a secretary on another partner's leather couch. The feudal concept of droit du seigneur still held sway in law firms, investment banks, and large corporations. But there was blowback due to the stain they'd left on the couch. The firm's only female lawyer, a junior associate, was the brunt of a continuous flow of belittling sexist jokes, which she pretended to find amusing and which, even in those unenlightened days, repulsed me if only because of their lack of humor. Indeed, I continue to believe jokes should be funny, even though that has become a minority point of view, beaten out by the belief that they should be inoffensive.

A deservedly unpopular obese partner leaned too far back in his desk chair and fell over backward, becoming jammed between his desk and the rear wall of his office, and was unable to get up. Rather than help him, someone closed his door and turned on his office radio to muffle his screams for help. Many hours later, the late-night cleanup crew rescued him. Well, that actually was funny.

---

[18] In my defense, interviewing for law firm jobs was a tricky process. When asked how they differed from other firms, they all gave some version of the same thing: "We're more relaxed—*laid-back*, as you kids say—than they are. When walking in the office hallways, if clients aren't present, we're allowed to leave our suit jackets off. Also, we discourage attorneys from leaving their office doors closed unless they want privacy."

[19] One night, when working late, I snuck into the partners' john. It featured luxurious plush towels, marble tiles, a shower, a couch, and a sauna. Feeling like an interloper in a sultan's harem, I feared being skewered on a eunuch's scimitar. My mood improved, however, after a sauna and shower, even if I was disappointed that there wasn't a masseuse on night duty.

A slovenly litigation partner, whose tie always looked like it had been tied by a pet squirrel, sent an associate to a Bumfuck, Indiana, warehouse to spend several days reviewing documents in connection with a pending lawsuit. Turned out there were fewer relevant documents than anticipated, so he came home early . . . only to find the partner in bed with his wife. The firm retained the partner and fired the associate on the theory that you *can't expect them to harmoniously work together after that.* The partner controlled business; the associate didn't.

One of the firm's lawyers asked me to forge a client's name to an SEC filing. I refused and, at his suggestion, left the room for ten minutes. When I returned, the client's signature had appeared at the base of the document, and a secretary had notarized it. In discussing litigation strategies, he'd use the expression "we could take the position that . . ." as a synonym for "let's lie." The firm knew about his dishonesty, but he brought significant business into the firm; and hey, no one was perfect. Decades later, he was disbarred for notarizing a client's signature on a crucial document on a certain date that turned out to be two days after the man, unbeknownst to the lawyer, had died.

One weekend, I spent two straight all-nighters working on a memorandum of law in support of an emergency motion. I thought I'd done a bang-up job. But when I, bleary-eyed, handed it to the partner, he tossed it in the trash, telling me the case had been settled Friday morning. He hadn't had a chance to tell me as he'd had to gather together his family and get on the road before the traffic on the way out to the Hamptons became intolerable. I asked that he at least read it, but he said, "I can't bill for that. It's enough that we're billing for your time over the weekend." He must've noticed my disappointment as he added, "You'll understand when you become a partner." Precocious as always, I didn't need to take that long to understand that he was a scumbag.

One positive thing, I did some work for Robert Kennedy's former speechwriter, who gave me an invaluable piece of advice: "Writing is rewriting." It may not sound like much, but I took it to heart, and it made me the writer I am today. So if you're unimpressed with what you've been reading, blame Adam Walinsky.[20]

Maybe it wouldn't have made much of a difference if I'd done a thorough job of investigating firms when I was interviewing. When I compared my experiences at the firm with those of my law school buddies, they told me that theirs had been roughly similar, although the details differed. Many of my friends worked for lawyers who periodically screamed at them for even the most minor screwups— even those of the partners themselves, who saw no reason to accept blame when they could pin it on underlings—and sometimes threw pens and other objects at them. Unfortunately, my dad had been onto something when he'd said, "A law firm is a collection of perfectly nice people who, put together, make one big bastard"—except that many of the partners didn't start out as such nice people. Many law firm partners, having endured similar hazing when they were junior lawyers, romanticized mistreatment of associates as a rite of passage, a kind of hazing. In those pre-#MeToo days, employee abuse was accepted as not merely a fact of life but also a perk of partnership almost on par with sexual harassment and a corner office. Partners, at least those who controlled a substantial book of business, enjoyed

---

[20] Over the years, some pieces of advice have stuck with me, while others, which may be equally good or better, floated by like windblown dandelion fuzz. A couple decades ago, a mediocre college tennis player, who worked on court maintenance and assisted with the young children's clinics, suggested that I hit the ball more in front of my body. That tip improved my game and continues to do so. Other advice from more esteemed pros never clicked with me.

virtually unfettered power. As Lord Acton observed 150 years ago, "Power tends to corrupt; absolute power corrupts absolutely." Put another way, give someone the opportunity to be an asshole, and he'll either jump at the chance or, if a decent person, grow into the role by a series of seemingly inconsequential steps.

My work at the firm primarily consisted of proofreading deal documents and doing *due diligence*, which entailed checking invoices against lists of computer equipment to ensure that the equipment being sold as part of tax shelter transactions actually existed, at least on paper. No legal training was necessary for such tedious scut work, which added little value but allowed the firm to pump up their invoices with unnecessary billed hours.

One of the firm's associates[21] billed one and a half times the number of hours he actually put in on the rationalization that he "worked very intensely"—a fraud from which the firm was happy to profit. Then there was the legendary associate, at another firm, who'd billed twenty-seven hours in a single day. He'd gotten in the extra three hours by working on an airplane from New York to Los Angeles and taking advantage of the change in time zones.

Serving as the lickspittle of arrogant law firm partners wasn't the life I'd imagined for myself back when I was a hip, radical young law student. Prone to careless mistakes and not understanding what was expected of me, I also wasn't the associate the partners had imagined for themselves.

Amy recently diagnosed me as suffering from ADHD, but that can't be true since it hadn't been invented until I reached middle

---

[21] As that associate, like many of the firm's ambitious strivers, rarely took vacations, I was surprised when he took off for a full week. Turned out he went to a town near Hudson Bay, so remote it took three full days of travel to get there, in order to view a total solar eclipse. I asked him how it was. "Cloudy," he replied.

age. It's just coincidental that I'm plagued by carelessness and lack of attention to detail,[22] restlessness, edginess, difficulty keeping quiet, and a compulsion to speak out of turn. Those traits made me a mediocre associate. I eventually learned to cover for my mistakes and undo them before anyone noticed, but by then, it was too late to salvage my career as a law firm associate.

When Larry Kasdan visited me in New York (back before he'd achieved the success that made him too superior to hang out with me and our other frat brothers), he spared no words in expressing how appalled he was by my "dreary, hermetically sealed existence" and how far I'd sunk from when I regularly spouted witticisms and felicitous turns of phrase that he'd eventually be happy to claim as his own. His comments drove home to me the full extent of my unhappiness with my job, which, in accordance with my commitment to the unexamined life, I'd been struggling to ignore.

The firm culture repulsed me, and I saw no opportunity for advancement to the rank of partner.[23] However, I didn't leave the profession because, when I was researching the law and drafting research memos, I enjoyed the work and even took masochistic pleasure in the occasional all-nighter and didn't know what else to do. To this day, I enjoy drafting legal papers. It's like working through a complex puzzle, although unlike crosswords and the like, I'm good at it and get paid for it. It's satisfying to find just the right word and craft a persuasive argument, and it's easier than writing fiction because there's no need to make things up. Lazy, unskilled lawyers lie. Good ones twist the facts until, barely recognizable, they support their case.

---

[22] Any typos and misspellings that you find in this autobiography aren't actually mistakes but have been intentionally inserted for verisimilitude.

[23] I assured myself that if ever given the power to be an asshole, I'd resist due to my thus far well-disguised strength of character. I can only hope my former secretaries, associates, and paralegals never write their autobiographies.

The first firm I worked for and the New York large law firm culture, in general, deserve my criticism. If, however, I'd recognized and controlled my carelessness and lack of attention to detail, as I eventually learned to do, I'd have been a better and happier associate—might even have received better treatment and more respect and maybe have become a wealthy, successful partner. Then I'd have been so insufferably arrogant that my autobiography would be unreadable.

At a lecture on criminal law, I met the featured speaker, John Iannuzzi—the only partner in the firm of Iannuzzi, Iannuzzi, and Iannuzzi, which he ran with two secretaries, Carmen and Aida. After making criminal law sound like fun (he was not only a charming raconteur but also the author of several novels based on his achingly handsome alter ego's experience as a crusader for justice, defender of the downtrodden, and irresistible chick magnet), he offered me a job. Turned out his practice was primarily devoted to defending Mafia-connected cigarette smugglers with a smattering of personal injury cases where doctors received kickbacks to exaggerate clients' disabilities. With a long face and long, thin nose, he resembled a bird of prey. A self-centered egotist and abusive screamer, he was even nastier than most bosses. His hawklike eyes spotted my every error, and his raptor brain made up others. For example, he threw a book at me when I had the supposed poor judgment to show my office to a woman I was dating. "We're not here to impress your yuppie girlfriends." Then he docked my salary to pay for repairing the book I'd broken by ducking that it slammed into a wall.

While heroically defending the wrongly accused held a romantic appeal, getting small-time mobsters off on technicalities wasn't my idea of a satisfying career and wouldn't impress women. Also, he expected me to be able to handle a lawsuit on my own with little supervision and much after-the-fact second-guessing. Doing scut work for a large firm, however, had taught me little beyond how to run up billable hours. I could have learned, as I eventually did, but he was too impatient and volatile to give me the time—not that I wanted to become an expert at eating his shit or at representing low-level Mafiosi or people faking whiplash injuries.

After my stint as a criminal lawyer, I landed a job with one of the foremost firms representing clients in the then-booming record industry. The firm, for example, represented Kiss and Gene Simmons of the legendary giant tongue and Linda Ronstadt, on whom I had a minor crush after seeing her posed as a sexy Cub Scout on her album cover. The partners told outrageous, allegedly true, stories about some of the giants of rock. For example, during a break from an all-night contract negotiation, Mick Jagger and Ahmet Ertegun allegedly fucked underage boys on the firm conference room table. Keith Richards, who *Rolling Stone* magazine anointed as the rock star most likely to not live long enough to see 1980 due to his legendary drug abuse but is still going strong at seventy-nine, purportedly snorted his father's ashes. And Van Halen insisted that their contract contain a clause prohibiting brown M&M's in their dressing rooms. But the partners hated one another—not unusual as law firms are snake nests of jealousy, backbiting, and raging egos. In this case, however, the enmity led to the firm's breaking up soon after I joined it, leaving me unemployed and yet more disenchanted.

Next, I worked for a small firm, where I came into my own as a litigator, winning three cases in a single year that were reported on the front page of the *New York Law Journal*, an accomplishment few entire law firms could match. Since childhood, my degree of focus, and thus my competence, has varied inversely with the complexity of the task. In second grade, my teacher told my mother that if asked to multiply two five-figure numbers in my head, I'd always arrive at the correct answer. But with two-figure numbers, my results tended to be hit or miss. Thus, although a sloppy proofreader and a careless junior associate, I eventually trained myself to be a good trial lawyer and excellent legal strategist, negotiator, and drafter of legal papers—unlike most people, I'm totally objective in evaluating my competence.

I worked for the firm's litigation partner who was the world-champion manipulator of me. When I seemed to relax, he'd scream at me for letting him down. When he'd push me beyond the threshold of acceptable anger, he'd calm me by praising my work— all in service of squeezing the most hours he could out of me. One time, he'd gotten me so annoyed that I shoved open the door to my office with such force the doorknob punched a four-inch hole in the wall. *Oh shit, now I'm totally fucked.* My boss stuck his head into the room and calmly said, "Please call building maintenance about that."

When pitching new clients, he told, in minute detail, the story of how, during his vigorous and vicious cross-examination, the defendant's face suddenly turned red. Then he clutched his chest, started to stand, and keeled over, dead. Appalled at the time, I was no less appalled when, years later, he told me that he'd made up the tale to impress clients. That his story made a favorable impression on clients told me more than I'd wanted to know about the art of self-promotion in the service of bringing in business.

When I complained that I was juggling so many cases that I was concerned that I'd be unable to keep on top of all of them, he said, "You don't know what it's like to have it hard. I've got to go to several cocktail parties a week to drum up business so you'll have cases to work on."

"I'd be willing to take some of those parties off your hands," I said.

The firm rejected my demand that I be made partner. My boss told me he'd argued on my behalf, but his partners had refused to go along. According to him, I was collateral damage from a power struggle within the firm. The other partners objected to what they saw as his efforts to turn the firm's litigation practice into his personal fiefdom and power base, to the detriment of the firm's corporate and entertainment practices.[24] He claimed the senior partner of the firm was gay and set on promoting the associates who worked for him and shared his sexual predilections. I was too tone-deaf to the ins and outs of firm politics to know if that had been the real reason for the failure to promote me. Also, in those benighted days, my gaydar was nonfunctional. Yet I knew there was something amiss as the senior partner had the irritating habit of not giving me my biweekly paycheck until I asked for it and then dropping it on the floor by "mistake" so I'd have to bend down to pick it up, giving him a close-up view of my butt, which, in those days, was worth looking at—at least that was what a myopic woman once told me.

I was six years out of law school and about to be fired[25] from a dead-end job. A failure and a loser, I fell into a well-deserved borderline depression. Even stretching my talent at self-deception to its breaking point, I could no longer pretend to be hip, cool, or groovy.

---

[24] In later years, he became a friend and a source of business. Claiming I was the best associate he'd ever had, he periodically asked me to leave my firm and join him at his new firm.

[25] At law firms, the failure to make a senior associate a partner was akin to giving him notice.

Then I caught a break that could result in the reconsideration of my case to be made partner. A presumably straight corporate partner in the firm, for whom I'd done some work, invited me to go skiing for the weekend.

Purportedly an expert skier, he'd festooned his office walls with photos taken on ski vacations with ex-wives and now-alienated children. I thought I'd be able to keep up, however, as he was *really* old—probably even the fatal side of forty.

We drove up to Killington, Vermont, slept in a nondescript inn, and hit the slopes as soon as the lifts opened. We skied several runs together. Then he suggested we split up so he could work on his bump skiing technique without me holding him up.

When we reconvened two hours later, I suggested we ski Cascade, a double black diamond expert trail that had been in excellent condition when I'd skied it earlier. As we started down, I realized my mistake. The morning's coating of fresh powder had been skied off, leaving an icy crust. Not a total surprise. Ice is as prevalent in New England skiing as arrogance is among lawyers. There were no cutoffs, so the only way to go was downhill. Fine, it wasn't glare ice or blue ice—just crust. (Vermont skiers had as many words for *ice* as Eskimos purportedly had for *snow*.)

We started downhill skiing side by side. Then hitting a steep pitch faster than was advisable, he fell, somersaulting downhill and breaking his leg in three places.

He didn't overtly blame me. But a month later, when the firm declined to reconsider its decision and I told him I was leaving the firm, he didn't ask me to stay.

In those days, when not working, I'd wasted vast amounts of time chasing after women with my law school friend Frank and playing the role of his nice, but unattractive friend—or rather his caustic, less good-looking friend. He was one of the few people I've met who could be described without hyperbole as *larger-than-life*: tall, handsome, intelligent, charming, charismatic, and appreciative of my attempts at humor, as I was of his. I thought of him as my best friend and mostly overlooked his obnoxiousness, such as his habit of making up pet names for each of the women we dated, mainly focusing on their body parts or odd quirks. For example, he nicknamed a well-endowed woman, Melons, and one not so endowed, Dog Tits. Although that was decades before the discovery of microaggressions and the need for "safe spaces," I told him not to refer to anyone I dated that way. However, I enjoyed his company, and we had some great times together.

Frank had everything going for him and would have been successful in politics or whatever else he put his mind to if he hadn't had a screw loose. Although failing the bar exam on his first try, he landed a job with a politically connected law firm and then leveraged that experience to secure a plum position as counsel to Mayor Koch. But then he became convinced that the mayor wanted to get into his pants and intended to have him killed because he'd rejected the mayor's, undoubtedly nonexistent, sexual advances. While lying on the floor of his apartment with him (according to him, we needed to avoid sniper sight lines through his windows), I realized Koch had given him notice, and Frank had constructed an excuse to cover up for his having been fired.

Toward the end of my career as a legal associate, David Herman, my friend and neighbor from when we were growing up (the one I'd complained to my parents about bullying me when we were kids), fixed me up with Stephanie, a friend of a woman he was dating. We hit it off and started dating.

I was sharing an apartment with Peter, my best friend from high school, and she was living with her parents. Both of us were unhappy with those arrangements (Peter was the cleanliness nut who'd suggested we leave the Woodstock festival), so it seemed an easy step for us to get an apartment and live together. While a commitment, it wasn't a frightening one. Not only were we in love, but also the apartment was in my name, and she could always go back to living with her parents if things didn't work out.

While we were living together, Stephanie so wanted to marry me that she'd cry when anyone mentioned the M-word. I had no reason to doubt that all the relationship lacked from her point of view was my long-term commitment. Neither of us had realized that she'd unconsciously assumed marriage would transform me from an overstretched shithead working in a dreary, unsatisfying job that demanded long hours while struggling to retain my male friendships and playing sports. She believed that once we were married, I'd metamorphize into a doting hubby who'd subordinate all my interests to hers. I, on the other hand, assumed that with her liking living with me and now getting the commitment she'd wanted, there was no reason for me to change.

When I announced our engagement, the partner whose leg I'd broken said, "You'll regret it if you do, and you'll regret it if you don't." Although I found that off-putting at the time, I now suspect that that's true more often than not. The road not taken has a perfection that the one taken can never match.

After we'd lived together for three years, half that time as spouses, Stephanie abruptly left me without a coherent explanation.

She claimed she'd frequently told me she was unhappy, and I hadn't done anything to accommodate her. Sure, she'd had the occasional irrational fit of uncontrolled fury, but at least she didn't hit me as Ann had. When she had complained about something I did, or more likely failed to do, we'd talk it out and reach what I'd believed was a mutually agreeable accommodation. She later claimed that in those discussions, I was "being a lawyer," which meant that I committed the unpardonable sin of thinking logically and explaining my positions articulately. I won the battles but had lost the war when she walked out. So much for the only reasonably happy part of my life at the time.

During our time together, Stephanie and I spent many evenings with Frank, his revolving door of girlfriends, and, ultimately, his wife. When he and I went out drinking without our wives, he'd tell me to man up and not take shit from Stephanie, whom he diagnosed with the Britishism "barking mad." I defended her to him. But by repeatedly stiffening my spine and belittling her complaints, he caused me to take her complaints less seriously than I should have, thereby undermining my relationship with her, perhaps intentionally. When Stephanie left me and I needed a friend, he wasn't there for me because, according to him, it made his wife uncomfortable when he'd hang out with his single friends and she didn't like getting together with him and me when I didn't have a date. In the months after my divorce, I was too despondent to go out on dates; and that was the end of my friendship with Frank, who wasn't about to man up and not take shit when it came to dealing with his own wife. He was committed to his wife, their future children, and being a grown-up. I felt like Peter fucking Pan. Then he moved to Washington DC to work for the *Washington Post*, and I saw him only twice since then.

A week after he'd aced a full physical exam, when he was in his late fifties, Frank went out for his usual morning run, came home, and showered. An hour later, his wife found him crumpled up in the tub, dead from an acute myocardial infarction. By then, I no longer resented him for not being there when I needed him and had hoped that we'd one day rekindle our friendship. He was the second of my close companions to have died, and I took it hard. There have been more since, and it hasn't gotten easier. Death is so unpleasantly final.

Recently, his wife called me after we hadn't spoken for fifteen years and talked about all the great times we three had together. It was delightful hearing from her. I felt guilty about writing what you've just read. Maybe my feelings of rejection were misplaced. But I didn't delete the previous paragraphs. It's my autobiography and my feelings, fucked up though they may be.

After Stephanie left me, I fell into a borderline depression, which from time to time morphed into a full depression. For some time, I didn't do anything to pull out of it because despondency felt like a reasonable response to my situation; and anyway, I had no idea what to do. At thirty-one, I was a failure abandoned by my wife and best friend and had no reasonable opportunity to turn things around. Ultimately, though, on the questionable theory that it was better to do something than nothing, I chose to do something stupid that virtually guaranteed to deepen my misery.

XVII

He Led Three Lives

1981

After the series of unpleasant and ultimately unsuccessful experiences working for law firms, I decided that working for other people wasn't for me—a conclusion with which most of my employers would have concurred with unseemly enthusiasm. I asked several of my law school friends if they'd like to form a firm with me, but they all told me that they didn't aspire to penury. So in desperation, I put a classified ad in the *New York Law Journal*, looking for corporate lawyers who needed a litigation partner to service their clients. No one, however, wanted to take in a partner without his own book of business. I became so desperate I considered looking for a job as an associate at a law firm, but I'd reached the stage of my career when no one wanted me unless I could bring in clients. They could easily hire a younger lawyer they could exploit without the risk of him demanding a share of the profits.

That is until I met James Harrison Cohen. In our discussions about forming a law firm, he assured me his connections generated significant litigation, which required an experienced litigator to handle. While JHC and I were finalizing our arrangement, he'd charmed David Ferber into joining us. Persuading me to join him was no great accomplishment as I had no other opportunities. But enticing David, a corporate lawyer with a substantial practice, to leave his partnership at a successful firm had taken months of sitting on the bathroom floor while David bathed his infant son and bringing David's wife flowers, well-chosen bottles of wine, and extravagant compliments.

As David and I later realized, JHC was single-mindedly pursuing partners in a last-ditch scheme to counter the centrifugal forces that were tearing his life apart. Rather than needing lawyers to handle his litigation and corporate work, he wanted suckers to share the expenses of the office, give him a veneer of respectability, and refer their clients to him so he could rip them off.

JHC led three parallel lives. In one, he was Harrison, a Harvard Law School graduate, member of the vestry of the Episcopal Church of St. James, and a former associate at a prestigious Wall Street law firm. He wore his straight black hair short; and with his pale, waxy, poreless skin, he resembled the horizontal guy at a funeral. With his rumpled dark suits and white shirts frayed at the collars and cuffs, he aped the shabby gentility of those with inherited wealth and family connections who had no need to impress others. As an eligible bachelor, he attended tony social functions and dated well-connected aristocratic blonde horse-faced equestrians. I didn't know what to make of his Sutton Place apartment with its chintz-covered couches, matching window treatments, and an antique étagère displaying an extensive collection of Meisel porcelain figurines. But always conscious of the image he projected, he'd designed the place to project a certain image, whatever that might've been.

As Cohen, he was the Jewish son of a politically connected Brooklyn judge. His dad, who was ultimately disbarred, had been a minion of Carmine DeSapio, the last head of the corrupt Tammany Hall political machine. So Cohen's political connections weren't fully kosher. Although amused by the contrast between his political fixer persona and his society lawyer persona, I told him I wouldn't be involved in anything improper. He assured me he wouldn't either but added that, for a lawyer, political connections are nothing to sneeze at. Unfortunately, I was allergic.

As a political fixer, he wore striped dress shirts and loud-patterned ties that clashed with his plaid suits, and he somehow managed to transform his appearance. The dark circles under his eyes looked like parentheses too tired to stand up, and his perpetual five-o'clock shadow gave his face a Roy Cohn–like lupine cast. His own practice concentrated on trusts and estates law, for which he wore somber black suits, starched white shirts, and subtly patterned ties. He billed for attending funerals, which seemed in bad taste.

The problem was his third life—as Jimmy, which he'd initially hidden from us and which involved cocaine, rough sex with underage boys, and a lifestyle that outstripped his legitimate income. In this persona, he dressed in metal-studded leather jackets and skintight leather pants and developed a variety of intimidating scowls à la Billy Idol. He took long vacations to exotic locales, returning looking more worn-out than when he'd left. He claimed he wasn't gay, just attracted to people under eighteen—all of whom just happened to be male. That explanation gave me little comfort. Further, from time to time, he showed up at the office with nasty bruises and black eyes courtesy of the recipients of his unwanted advances or the irate fathers of his sexual partners.

JHC, David, and I had been together for a few weeks when David and I learned that Jimmy had stolen escrow funds—the shortest route a lawyer could take to disbarment. We threw him out and changed the locks on the door. He responded by sending us postcards showing the entrance to Auschwitz with its infamous slogan *Arbeit macht frei* and the handwritten message "Wish you were here." An inauspicious start, but I'd never have met David and certainly wouldn't have been able to persuade him to be my partner if JHC hadn't devoted his sociopathic[26] charm to convincing him to join us.

A lithe marathon runner and an outgoing, loquacious family man with two young children, David Ferber was an incurable optimist. For example, when he bought a computer for the office, he told the manager of the electronics store that he was forming a law firm and gave him his card. He returned to the office claiming he'd landed a new client. Ten times out of ten, the potential clients he'd thought he'd charmed into retaining us wouldn't materialize, but I gave him credit for trying. It must be nice to be optimistic, not that I would know anything about that.

As a junior partner who was working on matters that the senior partner had brought in, David's prospects for professional and financial advancement had been limited. JHC convinced him that he'd improve those prospects by starting a firm with us, where he'd be able to retain all profits from the clients he could poach from his current firm. Thus, when JHC finally succeeded in convincing him to join us, David brought with him a substantial book of business, which he'd purloined when he left his former firm. Also, he had a very social, well-connected wife, which helped.

---

[26] My spell-check objects to the word *sociopathic* on grounds of inclusiveness as it supposedly "implies mental health bias." Called out by a computer program, I need to own up to the fact that I'm biased against sociopaths. Seems wokeness has gone so far that the only ones properly subject to criticism are Jews, Israelis, great men in history who happened to have owned slaves, and straight white men in general.

In law firms, bringing in business is the primary basis for compensation. Billing time and doing excellent work barely count since talented hard workers can always be hired on the relative cheap. Conflicts between the business getters and those that do most of the actual work have doomed many a law firm. As lawyers' egos are even more inflated than those of normal people, they have an exaggerated idea of the value of their contributions to their firms relative to those of their partners.

Initially, David and I weren't true partners. We practiced under a firm name, but rather than divide profits between us, we kept what we earned from our own clients and shared the expenses of the office. I referred corporate business to him, the little I had; and he sent me the litigation he had, which wasn't much. We divided the receipts, one-third to the one who brought in the business and two-thirds to the person who'd worked on it. David's referrals and the small cases I brought in generated enough receipts to cover my share of the overhead with enough left over to barely cover my modest living expenses.

In my first trial since entering into the space-sharing arrangement, I represented the owner of several construction sites for future McDonald's branches who was being sued for nonpayment by a guard service he'd hired to monitor the properties after working hours. His defense was that they'd overcharged him because, after terminating the guard service, he'd rented guard dogs at a fraction of the cost. However, his admission that three days after renting the dogs, they were stolen undercut that defense.

In the second one, I represented David Ferber in a lawsuit resulting from water damage caused by overflow from his negligently maintained leaf-clogged terrace drain. The case went to trial only because David had less of an incentive to settle than did most litigants since I was representing him free of charge. I won the case, thus cementing my relationship with David and giving him a chance to see me in action so he could truthfully tout my services to his clients.

After we'd shared space and expenses for a year, during which we worked well together and became friends, David and I formed a proper partnership, Ferber Greilsheimer Chan & Essner—with Bill Greilsheimer, a corporate lawyer from a large firm, and Allen Essner, a tax lawyer from another large firm. Bill and David, who were seven years older than Allen and me, had been partners in large firms and thus had more developed practices than we did, which explains how we came up with the order of the partners' names.[27] David and Bill had some litigation business for me, but it still wasn't enough to keep me occupied. However, between their cases and mine, I was now earning as much as I'd made as an underpaid junior associate. My old boss had kept my contacts with clients to an absolute minimum and glommed to himself all the credit for my good work. So unlike David, Bill, and Allen, I couldn't take clients from my former firm.

Before joining up with JHC, I should've researched his background and examined his financial books. Then I'd have known that his claim that he had litigation business to send me was a Trumpian overstatement. At least I should've had a plan of how, as a young lawyer without any connections, I could develop my own business. Had I analyzed my situation, I'd have known that joining David and JHC could be professional suicide and forming Ferber

---

[27] In forming a firm, lawyers routinely argued about who will be in the partnership name and the order in which their names will be listed—the order being a marker of prestige. Of course, lawyers argue about most everything, even the extent to which they're argumentative.

Greilsheimer Chan & Essner would be almost equally problematic if I couldn't bring to the partnership a significant amount of litigation. Without that, I'd be a de facto associate working for David, Bill, and Allen, notwithstanding my title of partner. They weren't abusive or manipulative like my former bosses. By virtue of their control over the firm's business, however, they'd have power over me; and I was well aware of Lord Acton's axiom about power corrupting.

Making well-thought-out decisions about my future, however, was antithetical to the unexamined life. Sure, Einstein defined *insanity* as "doing the same thing over and over and expecting different results." But I wasn't about to take advice on how to manage my life from a physicist who couldn't even manage his own hair.

XVIII

The Lore of the Jungle

1982–1983

I'd learned a great deal of law, but now I needed to learn the lore and the business of litigation.

A lawsuit is a giant machine a litigant enters as a pig and comes out a sausage, and those operating the machine or even standing in its vicinity, get splattered with blood and offal.

The great majority of cases are settled, which means both sides have had to compromise. As a result, if a litigant is entirely in the right, he ends up with less than he's entitled to, significantly less after legal fees. Settlement is unsatisfying, sort of like the hoary sports adage that a tie is like kissing one's sister, and you've never even met my sister. I always second-guessed myself; could I have gotten more for my client if I'd pushed harder? Judges say the best settlements are those where both sides leave the table unhappy, ideally equally unhappy. Perhaps, but that creates a marketing problem for the litigators. In a business that depends on referrals and word of mouth (if you're not in a position to steal clients from your old firm and take them to a new one), how do you convince a client that the settlement had been a win resulting from your fabulous work?

Generally, neither side is completely in the right, so settlement could lead to a just result. But even then, when legal fees are taken into consideration, everyone loses except the lawyers. The lawyers often lose too as the personality traits of those who get into frequent litigation—competitiveness, rigidity, paranoia, and self-righteousness—overlap with those who take umbrage at having to pay legal bills or enjoy negotiating them down. Pursuing clients for fees is among the most distasteful part of the business. Lawyers want to fight *for* their clients, not *with* them.

The court administrators rate judges on the efficiency with which they clear cases—justice playing no role in those calculations. Conducting a trial could take weeks of a judge's time. However, it takes few judicial resources to wear down litigants with multiple purposeless court appearances and unexplained adjournments until cascading legal fees force a settlement. To be fair, if only for a change of pace, state courts' dockets are too busy for even competent judges to properly handle all the cases assigned to them. If you're looking for justice, you'd be better advised to play three-card monte with sidewalk hustlers. As I used to tell my clients, you get justice in heaven, if at all; here, we just strive for the best result net of legal fees. Clients always say they're litigating as a matter of principle. They're in the right and, therefore, have no reason to settle. But after they receive their first bill, settlement becomes a matter not of *principle*, but of *principal*. By then, however, their hooves have been fastened to the conveyor belt carrying them inexorably toward the sausage grinder. The litigator's job is to make the best of a bad situation, getting them off that conveyor belt while their bodies, if not their souls, are still largely intact.

Litigation is satisfying if you have an honest, deserving, well-heeled client; a skilled and ethical adversary; and a capable judge. I'd occasionally heard of litigators who pulled off that trifecta. But I dismissed that as an urban legend, like the huge blind albino man-eating alligators rumored to populate New York City's sewers—descendants of tiny reptiles that had been purchased as souvenirs from the circus and accidentally flushed down the toilet.

Thus, litigation is not about striving for justice and only peripherally about preparing for trial and tying cases. It's primarily about gaming the system and running up the other side's legal fees in order to gain settlement leverage. When involved in that game, it can be fun, challenging, and remunerative; just be sure not to think about the yawning gap between what you accomplished and justice—that is, avoid the examined life. An analogy is Wile E. Coyote running off a cliff. He's fine until he looks down—when he does, he crashes into the earth below, sustaining the kind of devastating injury only a cartoon character can survive. Note to self: no more trite, overused, threadbare analogies.

Having learned the game, I eventually developed a thriving practice, but it wasn't easy. Much of the time, I felt like I was riding a mule in the Kentucky Derby of life.

XIX

The Law Is a Jealous Mistress[28]

1983–2010

I never knew where my next case would come from, except I eventually learned that it never came from where I expected. Just the same, the cases did come.

A law school friend, after being fired by the law firm for which he worked, became a successful agent for the licensing of trademarks and intellectual property under the ill-advised name the What Have You Done for Me Lately Company. His clients were happy to sign representation agreements with him, but unhappy to pay his commissions after he'd closed a deal for them and they no longer needed him. Also, he insisted on drafting his own representation agreements. If he had been any good at contract drafting, the firm he'd worked for wouldn't have fired him, so his contracts were replete with ambiguities subject to several interpretations. As a result, we ended up suing almost every client he ever had. I made him enough money from our lawsuits for him to buy a hundred-acre estate complete with stables, a riding ring, a swimming pool, and

---

[28] Supreme Court Justice Joseph Story's statement "The law is a jealous mistress and requires long and constant courtship. It is not to be won by trifling favors, but by lavish homage" has been often quoted by sadistic law professors and law firm partners to justify their demands that their underlings put in excessive billable hours to the detriment of their marriages, children, and sex lives.

a wine cellar worthy of a three-star restaurant. I did fine from the arrangement but never made enough to acquire such accoutrements, not that I wanted them. One of the partners in the first firm I worked for used to say, "Oh god, please let me come back as a client." His clients undoubtedly ended up wishing that those prayers had been answered so they'd end up with a different lawyer.

Once, I tried a case before a jury and then handled the appeal—both of which I inexplicably lost—against a partner in a huge law firm. One of several low points of the trial was when his client claimed mine had threatened to skin him alive and make lampshades out of his skin. My adversary and I became close friends, and he ended up referring matters to me where the amounts in issue were too small for his firm to handle economically but fine for me with my firm's lower overhead structure.

Four decades after we graduated, a high school friend, whom I'd voted for in his unsuccessful campaign for classmate "Most Likely to Succeed,"[29] referred to me a company that became my largest client. Now that I'm semiretired, I represent that client working part-time. Like Tom Hagen in *The Godfather*, "I have a special practice. I handle one client."

Most of my clients were happy with the work I did for them. Some, though, saw life as a zero-sum game and thought I was such an exceptional lawyer that they wanted to keep me to themselves so they'd have a leg up on the rest of the world. However, others (the promoter or salesman types) liked recommending people, whether they were lawyers, doctors, stockbrokers, housekeepers, shoeshine boys, or hookers; and those types referred clients to me with

---

[29] That election must've been fixed as I didn't win for "Best Sense of Humor."

sufficient regularity that I could earn a good living. In my second year on my own, I earned as much as a junior partner in a large firm. In the late '90s and the beginning of the current century, however, the compensation at the largest firms grew at a far faster rate than mine. But I was having more fun than them building my firm and going against those Biglaw[30] lawyers and beating them.

One such promoter client was Ira. He persuaded me to hire his wife as a paralegal. In her second week of work, after pledging me to secrecy, she asked for a day off because she was packing up to leave Ira. She was oblivious to the uncomfortable position she'd put me in. A stockbroker, Ira bragged that he'd never recommend to a customer a stock he didn't buy himself. That didn't work out all too well for him or his customers. Years later, I learned from Janet—by coincidence, one of his passengers—that he was driving a cab; and running into his ex, I learned he was living in that cab.

Clients always lie, but it seemed that mine lied more than most. It was as if they thought that because I was such a gifted litigator, fairness dictated that they give me a handicap to make things even. After mucking out the Augean stables of bullshit, I could generally determine how an intelligent, hardworking judge would decide a case. That would have been a pointless exercise, however, as the odds of having such a judge, in state court, were as remote as the chances of suffocating because all the oxygen molecules stuffed themselves into one corner of the room due to random Brownian motion. Nominated by the party machine for reasons other than intelligence, judicial temperament, or capacity for hard work, judges in New York State then run unopposed, often appearing on the ballot

---

[30] A term for describing the biggest and most prestigious law firms in the United States

simultaneously in each of the Democrat, Republican, conservative, and liberal party columns. As a result, having the typical state court judge correctly decide a complex commercial case is a roll of the dice.[31]

Once, in the early days of my partnership, I returned from a bruising day in court complaining about the idiotic judge I'd appeared before. My partner Bill Greilsheimer responded, "Your job is to persuade the stupid judges." He had a point.

While it seems to clients that cases go on forever, they all do end, often with an unexpected settlement. The most wearying part of running a litigation practice is the constant need to bring in new cases just to replace the ones that ended. As my firm grew, largely due to my efforts, I had to bring in sufficient business to pay the salaries of ten people as well as rent, taxes, etc. before I could take out a cent for myself. While I ultimately did fine financially, whenever the case flow slowed, I feared I'd be out of business. At the end of each year, I'd tell friends, "I had a good year, but next year looks awful." They'd respond that they'd heard me say the same thing the previous year, and I shouldn't worry because business had always come in and most likely would continue to do so. But I believed that if I slacked off, business would collapse and never recover. I didn't know if that was true as I never slacked off. Living off the business I brought into the firm, my partners prided themselves on their relaxed attitude. Easy for them—they had me.

---

[31] Appearing in Federal court is a far superior experience. The quality of the judges is higher. Not only are they, for the most part, chosen on the basis of merit but also they have a smaller caseload and smart, dedicated clerks. I've had many satisfying experiences in Federal court but I live by the adage that if you don't have anything critical and humorous to say about someone or something, don't bother saying anything.

As business trickled and then flooded in, I learned, from painful experience, that one of the most important things to know in running a litigation practice is what cases *not* to take. Many legitimate claims didn't involve enough money to justify the legal fees that would be required to do a competent professional job. Others involved clients who were so disreputable, obnoxious, or untrustworthy that I couldn't stomach working with them; and their horrendous reputations would negatively affect my own. Many of them were involved in litigation because they'd failed to honor their legal obligations and would continue that practice when it came to paying their lawyer. When business slowed, I was tempted to take cases I wouldn't have if I'd been busy, but that would have been a mistake. Cases linger; and the crap cases would still be requiring attention when business picked up and therefore would take up time that would be better devoted to more profitable cases or, for that matter, just screwing off.

Then there was the problem that deserving clients who'd suffered grave injustices made me uncomfortable. I'd worry about the litigation machine turning them into sausages, with my legal fees serving as the sausage casings. Also, the risk that I'd lose, if only due to the randomness of the shambolic system, kept me up at night. Deserving, honest clients turned out to not be such a big problem, though, as people who knew how to get along with others and who honored their legal and business obligations rarely got into litigation.

Among the cases I turned down or would have turned down if they'd come to me, was a claim for parenting malpractice that a teenager wanted to bring against his father. The boy had gotten feces on the back seat of his father's car from having anal sex with his girlfriend. When his father confronted him, he blamed his dog, whom his father proceeded to shoot. Then there was the claim by a deceased woman's parents who wanted to sue the boyfriend of their daughter who'd choked to death after swallowing his cell phone in an argument over his desire to take a call. And there was the woman who'd broken her leg having tripped over a bright yellow Caution Wet Floor / Piso Mojado sign. A similar case involved a woman who wanted to sue a restaurant because she'd slipped on a soft drink and broke her coccyx. The beverage had been on the floor because she'd thrown it at her boyfriend thirty seconds earlier during an argument over his failure to tell her how great she looked. Then there was the young investment banker who asked me to sue a strip club for allowing him to run up a six-figure tab on his firm's expense account by buying rounds of fake champagne for his fellow VIP room attendees. Then there was the head of a political party formed to counter Jewish / British / royal family world domination. That one was particularly easy to turn down as he wanted me to represent him, pro bono publico, because I'd be serving the public good, not that I'd bothered to find out what the case was about. I'd made it a practice not to represent paranoid anti-Semites free of charge—pro *malo* publico.

Oh, I almost forgot the lawyer/friend who asked me to represent his son. The young man, who claimed to suffer from attention deficit disorder, finagled an extra two hours for the bar exam as well as the special dispensation of being allowed to take it in his own quiet room—with just him and the proctor. In spite of these advantages, he failed the exam. The basis for his contemplated suit against the New York State Bar Association was that the proctor had dropped his pencil several times, thereby distracting him. If his son couldn't pass the bar exam under such favorable circumstances, I asked my friend, how could he practice law in a world full of distractions? After that, he and I didn't speak for decades.[32]

In one of my early cases, a tall muscular artist retained me to recover one of his paintings he'd loaned to a dominatrix, who intimidated him to such a degree that he was terrified of asking her to return it. I wrote her a demand letter, and she promptly agreed to return the painting. When she showed up at my office struggling to lug the ugly huge artwork, I had trouble retaining my laughter. Meek, respectful, and apologetic, she was barely five feet tall and couldn't have weighed more than one hundred pounds.

In another case, my client had been fired for telling a woman who worked for him to "bend your knees and blow."

"What motivated you to say something so offensive?" I asked him.

"She was lifting a heavy box, and that was what my father used to say to me so I'd avoid getting a hernia. I thought of offering to help her with the box, but I was afraid she'd consider that sexist."

I couldn't persuade his employer to keep him on. But at least I got him a respectable settlement package and, to my subsequent regret, kept him as a client.

Once, a law firm hired me to sue Trump to recover their legal fees. He owed the money and had no legitimate defense. He just refused to pay. After I filed suit and he saw that I wasn't going to cave in, he paid the entire amount. Not paying bills and forcing creditors to go through the expense and inconvenience of suing

---

[32] I recently ran into my former friend, who told me that although he was Jewish, he'd married an Episcopalian. She told him that she wished he'd convert so "we could be in heaven together." How could a bright, sophisticated woman believe that a god who created billions of Hindus, Catholics, and Buddhists would limit his heaven to a few million Episcopalians as if it were a WASPs-only exclusive country club?

was his modus operandi, one that he continued for the following four decades. That's just one of several reasons why those from his home state, who did business with him or even just know him despise him.

Four years after we started the firm, I met Barry Trupin, thanks to an introduction from Bill Greilsheimer; and as a result, I went from being a struggling young lawyer to being a well-known presence on the New York legal scene.

In the early '80s, the highest marginal federal tax rate was 70 percent, for an overall rate of over 80 percent if New York State and City taxes were included. With such elevated rates, tax avoidance proliferated, and the syndication of tax shelter deals became a huge lucrative business. Those deals were structured, via financial legerdemain, to throw off tax deductions several times larger than the amount the investor put into the deal. Nevertheless, the offering memoranda that described the deals disclosed that the IRS might disallow those deductions and hit the investors with substantial penalties and interest charges. With varying degrees of success, the promoters buried such disclosures in boilerplate. Their investors, blinkered by greed, didn't bother reading hundreds of pages of intentionally turgid legalese in the offering documents. Instead, they relied on their accountants and financial advisors to review the deals. In what seemed to the investors to be a good deal, their professionals often didn't charge them for their review. Instead, the promoters paid those fees, often along with undisclosed kickbacks when their clients invested in a transaction. As should've been obvious to the investors, this system motivated their advisors to put their own financial interests ahead of those of their clients. When their advisors told them to ignore the "risk factors" section of the offering memos, they were happy to do so. Who wants to read that crap anyway? Even I didn't, and I was being paid to do so.

In 1987, the tax law changed. The IRS became more aggressive, disallowing deductions from these deals. The investors sued, alleging that the promoters of the deals had defrauded them. Barry Trupin, one of the larger and more aggressive of these promoters, hired me to defend him.

He'd named his primary company Rothschild Reserve, although he had no connection to the real Rothschilds. He even mused on the possibility of suing them for using *his* name. He also used the name MHTC for one of his companies. He claimed he'd named it after his parents, Mildred and Harry Trupin, and that it was a coincidence that the giant Manufacturers Hanover Trust Company used the same initials in its logo. Sure, he was something of a con man, but he was my con man and intriguingly larger-than-life.

Barry purchased a mansion on the beach in Southampton, New York, the toniest of the Hamptons. Although sufficiently commodious for the du Pont family, who'd built it to show off their obscene wealth and questionable taste, it was inadequate for Barry, who began renovations with the intent of turning it into the largest private house in the history of the New York State. His guests would be able to picnic in an underwater grotto complete with a thirty-foot-tall waterfall cascading into an indoor saltwater swimming pool, well stocked with exotic tropical fish. They (the guests, not the fish) could then recline on Turkish pillows in a room that had been removed from an Ottoman palace and reconstructed on the second floor of his mansion, or they could drink in an actual pub transported from Liverpool. And those were just two of the castle's sixty-three rooms. He never finished the project, however, as the humorless Southampton Town Building Department shut down construction due to a record number of violations of the town's zoning code. When a hurricane threatened the South Shore of Long Island, TV news covered the cavalcade of Barry's eighteen vintage Rolls-Royces departing his villa for safety inland. It was fun to be part of that ludicrous excess. Incidentally, when you smile at a woman from the back seat of a Rolls, she smiles back.

His cases were perfect for me in the early stage of my career. While he deserved no sympathy, neither did the self-righteous pigs— mostly greedy, rich doctors—who'd invested with the intention of shortchanging the government and, ultimately, the American people. They were too lazy to review the offering memos themselves and too cheap to pay their accountants and financial advisors to review the deals on their behalf rather than on behalf of the promoters. Those investors knew or should have known that the IRS might disallow their deductions if it audited them. Indeed, all the investors would have needed to have done to inform themselves of the risks would have been to read the "risk factors" section in their offering memos. Although loaded down with boilerplate, the offering memos were legally required to set off the "risk factors" section in boldfaced type. With one pig pitted against another pig, no result would've made me feel guilty. Also, in each suit, the investors were suing for significant money; and if Barry were to lose any of the cases, that case would be a binding precedent against him in future cases. If he won a case, however, the precedent wouldn't preclude other investors from suing because they, unlike Barry, weren't parties to that proceeding. Thus, the money to mount a winning defense was no object. Unlike my usual cases, where high legal fees could not be justified in light of the amounts in issue, I could put in all the work necessary to do a first-rate job; and I was free to play whatever sly procedural gambits and clever litigation games that caught my fancy. Also, as Barry was being sued in cases all around the country, I had significant business travel. I enjoyed the change of pace from sitting all day in my office and made useful connections with the lawyers I'd retained as local counsel in the jurisdictions in which I wasn't admitted to the bar.

It occurred to me that I might not be on the side of the angels when, in answer to a question posed by a dinner date, I told her about the cases I was handling; and her face took on the expression of someone who'd swallowed a rotten oyster. After that revelation, I was left with two options: I could refuse to further represent Barry or do a better job of spinning my involvement to make me come off as a crusader for truth, justice, and the American way. I won't insult your intelligence by telling you which I chose.

Several years into my representation of Barry, I represented his wife in a lawsuit. When I picked her up in a cab to go to court, I held the door open for her. But she said, "The gentleman gets in first so the lady doesn't have to slide her ass across the seat." For her appearance before an Afro-American judge, she wore a sort of modified safari outfit complete with pith helmet and ostentatious jewelry. Nothing but class.

Ultimately, Barry and I had a falling-out over his failure to pay my legal fees—it wasn't personal, just business[33]. Deprived of my counsel, he went to jail for knowingly selling a forged Chagall. Since he'd bought it thinking it was authentic, it seemed fair to him to pass the loss on to another unsuspecting sucker once he learned it was a forgery. The US attorney, who already had it in for him due to the feds' failure to convict him of facilitating tax fraud, prosecuted him; and he was convicted of art fraud. I don't mean to imply that if I'd

[33] My former partner, Bob Kaplan, has a theory that everything in life can be explained or illustrated by a quote from *The Godfather*.

still represented him, he'd have been okay. He didn't always take my advice. Since he was richer than me, he thought he must be smarter. Now he's neither richer nor smarter.

One of my more interesting clients was Hakan, a seventeen-year-old NYU student and Turkish immigrant, who showed up in my office wearing a torn undershirt and filthy jeans, the peach fuzz on his cheeks unshaven. Not owning a wallet, he kept his cash in a ripped plastic bag that tended to leak pennies and the occasional dime. He had sad large brown eyes and a lost look that reminded me of a mistreated puppy, which made me want to protect him, hug him, and tell him everything would be all right. He came to me because a bank from which he'd borrowed a large sum of money had sued him based on allegedly fraudulent misrepresentations. Why had the bank loaned this pathetic, but inoffensive lost boy so much money? Surely, the claim that he'd misled the bank in his loan application was as phony as he claimed it to be. An easy case—all I needed to do was talk to the bank's lawyer and resolve what was clearly a misunderstanding.

As I learned more about Hakan, however, the matter became more complicated. He had a profound understanding of the investment world and could explain complex securities clearly and simply. I was astounded to learn he'd contributed $21 million to NYU. Laudatory front-page newspaper stories and magazine pieces touted him as a self-made boy genius who'd achieved fabulous investment returns for his clients, a group that included some of the biggest names in finance. He was the real thing, and I was proud to represent him.

As I got deeper into the case, however, the facts became fuzzy, like early versions of the dial-up internet, and then disappeared entirely, only to return in transmogrified form as chimeras whose lionlike jaws were intent on biting me in the ass. Postal inspectors looking into claims of credit card fraud discovered that the computers in Hakan's Greenwich, Connecticut, office weren't even plugged in and were as decorative as the ravishing women he'd hired to help him ravish his marks. Rather than being the naive idiot savant he'd at first appeared to be, Hakan was a sociopathic con man who'd run a Ponzi scheme, repaying old investors with money he'd scammed from new ones. NYU had to return the money it had received, only a fraction of the $21 million he'd promised them. The headlines were now far from laudatory: *New York Post*, May 11, 2005: "'Scam' Kid Has No Class; NYU 'Graduation' Fake"; May 22, 2005: "NYU 'Bank Scammer' in Tangled Web of Deception." A front-page article in *New York* magazine entitled "Mommy's Little Con Man" began, "When NYU senior Hakan Yalincak was arrested and put in jail after attempting to cash a forged $25 million check, his mother, Jackie, tearfully supplied a sketchy, convoluted explanation for everything. And when, a month later, she too was arrested for fraud, it seemed she'd taught her son everything she knew."

I'd managed to steer him through a series of civil cases, mostly by negotiating settlements that involved him giving back fraudulently obtained funds. Then he was indicted in Connecticut for wire fraud and other crimes. As I wasn't admitted in Connecticut and didn't practice criminal law, I couldn't represent him. Against my advice, he retained a self-promoting celebrity criminal lawyer, who, like many lawyers with big self-created reputations, paid insufficient attention to his client's needs. As a result, Hakan ended up pleading guilty to running a hedge fund scam and was sentenced to three and a half years in federal prison.

He was then deported to Turkey. Last I heard, he was living in Istanbul and studying law in England, where he'd failed to disclose his conviction on his school application. *Living in Istanbul and studying law in England?* Nothing about him made sense, and by then, I'd given up trying to understand.

Subsequently, his lawyer, Mickey Sherman, was publicly castigated for his inept representation of Kennedy relative Michael Skakel, whose murder conviction was later reversed on appeal on the ground that Sherman's representation had been inadequate. Sherman was later disbarred for tax fraud.

In a case blessedly devoid of moral content, I represented a member of the Saudi royal family, who, over drinks at the bar of the Four Seasons Hotel George V in Paris, had signed a contract obligating him to pay a €5 billion finder's fee. He hadn't bothered to read the contract or have a lawyer read it because the person he was dealing with had put his hand on his own neck while assuring my client that, contrary to the clear language of the contract, he'd have no personal liability as the contract was a meaningless formality. In Saudi Arabia, as my client explained to me, when someone makes such a gesture, symbolically putting his life on the line, he will honor it because if he didn't, no one would marry his sisters or daughters or buy his goats. To his profound disappointment and incredulity, I told him that under US law, people are expected to read what they sign, and the words of a contract take precedence over symbolic hand signals or oral representations.

We had to meet in person so that Bob Kaplan, my junior partner, and I could learn all relevant facts—something difficult to do telephonically, particularly if there are issues involving a different culture and clients with thick, sometimes hard-to-understand accents.[34] The client was uncomfortable coming to the United States since the last time he'd been there, the most attractive of his three wives had been strip-searched. I wasn't comfortable going to Saudi Arabia because my passport showed I'd been to Israel. So he flew me, Bob, and David Ferber, who insisted on tagging along, to Zurich to discuss the case. He put us up in sweet suites in a five-star hotel owned by one of his princely cousins. He also flew to Switzerland one of his favorite Rolls-Royces; two of his most valued bodyguards; two Saudi business associates, who had some knowledge about the background of the transaction; and the third of his current wives, a gorgeous, sophisticated multilingual Lebanese woman. She'd arrived with two suitcases and left with ten. I can't imagine what she'd filled them with. It takes a shitload of jewelry and haute couture to fill even one large Louis Vuitton suitcase. Perhaps she cornered the market on Swiss cheese and chocolate.

In his home country, my client wore ceremonial robes and didn't drink alcohol. In Switzerland, however, he wore jeans and Manchester United jerseys and was a Dionysian host. After multiple bottles of rare vintage Burgundy, followed by after-dinner snifters of Rémy Martin XO Excellence, we discussed the problems in the Middle East. He told me he admired Israel, although he mistakenly believed that it had an outsized influence on US foreign policy. He disliked the Palestinians, who, he said, "always had their hands out. Look at the difference between Jericho, a disgusting slum, and Tel Aviv, a prosperous city." With that as a start, he and I agreed on a resolution of the Israeli-Palestinian imbroglio. If we'd been authorized negotiators, the entire course of Middle Eastern history

---

[34] Not that *my* enunciation would present any difficulties. After all, God speaks English, as evidenced by the King James Bible, *Paradise Lost*, and *The History of the World, Part 1*.

would have taken a dramatic positive turn, and a professional writer would be composing my biography.

Bob Kaplan claimed that the reason a member of the Saudi aristocracy and I got along so well was that the princeling, with his rudimentary English, was attuned to my third-grade-level sense of humor. I may be flattering myself, but I hope you'll agree that my sense of humor is at least on the level of a dim-witted high school sophomore.

My client was such an endearing fellow that it was a shame he had such a bad case, but that was where the art of negotiation came in. I explained to my adversary that, while he may have a winning case, he'd have a hard time collecting on any judgment. All my client's assets were in Saudi Arabia, and if anyone were to try to enforce a judgment there, he was more likely to be beheaded than to collect. In that successful negotiating strategy, I'd played on my adversary's prejudice against Arabs, without basis in fact . . . probably. I settled the case for $50,000—a small percentage of the legal fees it would have cost him for me to try the case and ultimately lose €5 billion.

One of my more satisfying trials involved the fraudulent sale of a classic Formula 1 race car to a pal of Mark, my fraternity brother whom I'd drag-raced against in college. The case wasn't all that interesting. But my former boss, John Iannuzzi, was on the other side; and I outlawyered him, beating him handily.

In spite of my anxiety when representing the rare clients who were in the right, I did have some cases where I was on the side of the angels. In one, where I made a substantial positive difference in someone's life, I represented a woman who'd advised the Blue Man

Group when they were putting their act together. She claimed she'd been their de facto director, although she was not listed as such, and the producers downplayed her contribution. They contended that, therefore, she wasn't entitled to a percentage of their receipts under the Stage Directors and Choreographers union contract. I got the Blue Men to testify on her behalf, and the jury ruled in her favor. Now four decades later, she's still receiving substantial royalties, which she used to reinvent herself as a therapist for battered women.

A tax lawyer friend of my high school friend Peter referred to me a brilliant investment analyst and strategist with several degrees from Harvard and a Ph.D. from MIT who was the son-in-law of Sun Myung Moon. A self-proclaimed messiah and messenger of Jesus Christ, Moon was the founder of the multimillion-member Unification Church, which he'd built into a multibillion-dollar transcontinental business empire. Accordingly, in addition to my client's prodigious intelligence and impressive investment track record, he had impeccable access to wealth, power, and an inexhaustible supply of gullible Moonies. He could hardly have been in a better position to develop a lucrative wealth management business.

He'd retained me to defend him in a suit to enforce a promissory note he'd signed that the tax lawyer had drafted. The document was so complex that no judge could follow its byzantine procedure for enforcement, so I settled the case for pennies on the dollar.

It took me a while to figure out why such a well-connected and talented person had gotten himself into such severe financial difficulties that he'd defaulted on a loan. The answer can be summed up in a single word: cocaine. But he swore to me that, after a stint in a fancy clinic, he'd gotten clean and now had a fabulous opportunity to expand his wealth management business. He'd formed a partnership with a good-looking, smooth-talking Yale Law School graduate who was the well-connected son of the then-senior senator from Delaware.

This dream team, however, turned into a nightmare due in part to Hunter Biden's self-regard and lack of management ability. Also, my client hadn't been as clean as he'd claimed to be. Surprisingly enough, cocaine usage hadn't enhanced either party's performance or judgment. Their shambolic management led to investor complaints and possible regulatory investigations, which I successfully dealt with, and I negotiated and resolved several problems that would otherwise have resulted in futile litigation between my client and Hunter.

I thought I'd gotten the business back on track as both my client and Hunter seemed to have cleaned themselves up. However, a new problem arose that I was incapable of solving. My client's wife had an affair with the guitarist of the Unification Church band, which resulted in a child—the end of her marriage to my client and the concomitant loss of his connection to the church and its potential investor members. The business went kaput.

Last I heard, my former client was involved in an Amway-style multilayered marketing pyramid scheme featuring a drink made from an obscure tropical fruit he touted as a cure for everything from obesity to cancer. As for Hunter, well, we've all heard too damn much about him recently.

The big cases were easy. The huge firms on the other side assembled teams of dozens of lawyers and at least an equal number of paralegals and other support staff. With so many people handling the matter, no one person was as familiar with the case as I was, and their unconscionable legal fees made it less expensive for their clients to fork up massive settlement payments than to pay the fees that they'd incur if the case went to trial. For example, I represented a good-looking man who'd married the daughter of a billionaire and, on the strength of that relationship and his supposed ability to bring in investors, talked himself into a partnership with two real estate developers and a self-described star architect—a *starchitect* in real estate parlance. He, however, failed to generate investors; and then his wife filed for divorce, cutting off his access to her father and his wealthy pals. His partners brought an arbitration seeking to have him thrown out of their firm, alleging that he'd misrepresented his ability to bring in investors and failed to make a positive contribution to the management of the company. The dispute concluded in a week-and-a-half-long arbitration. Davis Polk, the huge law firm on the other side, utilized twenty-eight-time billers (whom my spell check identified as time *bilkers*) and, in the process, ran up fees in excess of $3 million. In contrast, my fees (for my work with Bob Kaplan and a paralegal) were under $750,000—a huge fee from my perspective. Oh, and I won the case, with the other side having to pay my client's legal fees. Too bad I hadn't billed more.

Due to good impressions I made on some of my adversaries and their clients and recommendations from my own clients, I developed a thriving practice, which included large European banks and financial institutions as well as celebrities such as Jay-Z and lawsuits involving John Grisham and Björn Borg.[35]

---

[35] While I'm concerned that my rendition of my single life, in the following chapter, might come off as bragging about my erotic adventures, in spite of my repeated failures in that area, I have no such concern about my legal abilities. I'm a damn good lawyer, and I'm not shy about telling anyone who'll listen about it. That reminds me of Churchill's responses when told that his unprepossessing political opponent Clement Attlee was a modest man: "a modest man with much to be modest about" and "a sheep in sheep's clothing."

My case for rap star and businessman Jay-Z case involved a dispute over a commercial real estate deal that went bad. The case against John Grisham grew out of the author's efforts to weasel out of the ongoing contractual obligations he owed to his agent. Trying to telephone the agent one night, he'd reached the agent's live-in male lover—thereby discovering, to his disgust and dismay, that not only had the agent had the bad judgment to die but also, even worse, had been gay. That resulted in two simultaneous cases: He brought one in federal court in Oxford, Mississippi, to avoid paying his agent's estate on deals the agent had found for him before he died that were still generating massive royalties. I'd brought the other in federal court in New York seeking to enforce those ongoing contractual obligations. It doesn't take extraordinary legal perspicacity to realize I'd be better off representing a dead elderly gay Jewish guy in New York City than in Mississippi. So I made a motion to have the Mississippi case transferred to New York and combined with the case I'd filed. A much-admired local son of Mississippi, Grisham moved to have the New York case transferred to Mississippi and combined with the case he'd filed in his home state. As I'd filed the first suit, I'd succeed in having both cases heard in New York if I could show that Grisham had sufficient contacts with New York State to justify proceeding in that state. We prevailed because I demonstrated that he'd taken numerous trips to New York to meet with his publisher, giving New York a legally sufficient basis to assert jurisdiction.

Although he'd banked over a hundred million bucks in royalties from his books and the movies made from them and owned a thousand-acre horse-breeding farm in Virginia and his own jet, he testified that he loved coming to New York because the publisher paid for his hotel room at the Plaza. With all that money, it seemed crazy to come to New York just to take advantage of a comped hotel room. However, everyone is crazy when it comes to money. I've known rich people who'd walk rather than spend a couple of bucks to take the subway and poor people who felt pinched only when they'd run out of people to hit up for loans. People who don't appear to you to be out of their gourds when it comes to money don't seem to be nuts only because they have the same neurosis about money that you do.

In the case against the legendary tennis great Björn Borg, I represented a self-important spendthrift—the one who, years earlier, I'd represented when he'd lost a job for telling his female subordinate "bend your knees and blow" and who now managed and ran into the ground Borg's men's clothing venture. Although not the brightest witness I'd ever deposed, Borg was the most focused. Even in the unfamiliar world of litigation, the concentration and mental toughness that had made him one of the all-time great tennis players came through. In contrast to my arrogant, thin-skinned client, Borg was also a nice guy. He invited me to hit with him at Tennisport, a club in Long Island City to which I belonged and where he played when he was in New York. We both knew it would never come about, but it was good of him to offer. Too bad he missed out on the opportunity to benefit from my comments on how to improve his serve and backhand. And the case? My client fired me when I told him he didn't stand a chance and we should settle.

Over time, I learned the essential art of client management and something of the art of negotiation.

Once, a client asked for a discount on my fee.

"Well, let's first go over what you're hiring me to do," I said. "You expect me to draft brilliant pleadings and briefs, take depositions, review and analyze discovery documents, and try the cases if necessary but more likely to negotiate settlement. Right?"

"Sure, but—"

"And I need you to have confidence in my abilities. Yes?"

"Of course, but about the discount."

"If I let you beat me in a negotiation, it will undermine that confidence. That's why my rates will remain unchanged."

He laughed and wrote a check.

Toward the end of a long trial, he asked me to write out my summation in advance and read it to him, for comment. When I did, he said, "That was terrific. I couldn't have done better myself."

Of course, he couldn't have for the same reason why I couldn't have run his company as well as he did or why a sociopath who played a businessman on a scripted reality show wouldn't make a better president than an experienced politician who understood the ins and outs of Washington or, for that matter, anyone with a heartbeat.

When he asked me to make changes in a brief I'd written (after reading this, it may come as a surprise to you that I wrote superb, even poetic briefs), I said, "If you hired a brain surgeon, would you tell him where to cut? Leave me alone to do my job. Your job with respect to this case is limited to paying me promptly."

After I won his case and he no longer needed me, he stiffed me on my final bill. That was okay as I'd inflated my bills sufficiently to take into account that eventuality and make room for a courtesy refund if he happened to pay in full. A lawyer who hasn't learned to protect himself probably won't do a good job protecting his clients.

But that goes only so far. A woman once asked me to recommend the most vicious lawyer I knew—one who, unlike me, wouldn't be restrained by legal niceties. So I did. She subsequently called irate that he'd overcharged her and gotten sanctioned by the court for improper conduct. I replied, "You requested a vicious lawyer unconstrained by legal niceties. Seems I gave you just what you asked for."

Clients brought in by corporate/securities partners David Ferber and Bill Greilsheimer[36] and, to a lesser extent, tax partner Allen Essner initially formed the backbone of the firm. As time went on, however, the value of my contribution increased, while theirs stagnated. Based on a compensation system that gave them credit for the proceeds from clients they'd originally brought into the firm, David and Bill continued to take substantially more money out of the firm than I did, notwithstanding the fact that I'd been solely responsible not only for doing the legal work but also for maintaining and developing the relationships with those clients. Most gallingly, any business I brought in as a result of contacts I'd made while representing those clients, even including referrals from former adversaries who never met David or Bill, and even referrals from those referrals were treated as David's or Bill's for compensation purposes.

Naturally, I came to resent that David and Bill were taking far more out of the firm than I was even though, by any economically

---

[36] Greilsheimer was so cheap that he attempted to help finance his kids' college education by having his whole family scour the sidewalks for inadvertently dropped coins, and he screamed at me for writing notes to myself on pages from printed "while you were out" pads rather than less expensive blank paper. A genius in his way, he was so knowledgeable in the most recondite and theoretical aspects of the law that his expertise blinded him to real-world practicalities. Such practicalities included the fact that judges, being less facile at resolving complicated legal issues than he was, would issue rulings that didn't conform to his view of the law. He couldn't see the forest for the tiny crenulations in the bark of a certain tree.

sensible measure,[37] I contributed more to the bottom line than they did. I was not only putting in more hours but also supervising the work of several lawyers and paralegals. Equally naturally, they resented my efforts to renegotiate our compensation arrangement. According to an old adage, hell has no fury greater than a lawyer scorned. Did I get that right? Oh, never mind.

In the last few years of our partnership, I finally succeeded in reshaping the firm's compensation system. As a result, I was making a multiple of what David made. Finally, my compensation again matched that of Biglaw junior partners. As far as accumulating points in the game, I was doing well—a fact of which I was inordinately proud. David also made out well in the deal as he got to enjoy resenting me.

When David and I eventually had a major blowup, as described below, I overreacted. Unfortunate, but no surprise given human nature.

Building a successful law firm had revitalized my life. Although short on connections, charm, hair, and stature, I impressed people with my intelligence, wit, aggressiveness, and desperation. Being a pugnacious shithead was a positive adaptation to my career. I got a thrill from bringing in new cases; gloried in my victories, which far outnumbered my defeats; took satisfaction from having made a material positive difference in the lives of some clients; relished many of my relationships with clients, coworkers, and even some of my adversaries; and mostly enjoyed the practice of law, particularly

---

[37] In this context, *sensible measure* means one that results in increasing my compensation and decreasing theirs. Had I been living an examined life, I might have defined the phrase differently. That, though, would have been a mistake as there's no profit in being the only reasonable person in a group.

when drafting complex legal papers or negotiating settlements of seemingly intractable disputes.

The nineteenth-century British writer Rudyard Kipling characterized success and failure as "two impostors" to be treated "just the same." Easy for him to say once he became a success. In my case, going from being mired in the misery of self-perceived failure to strutting along the sunny uplands of self-defined success wasn't merely a change in exterior circumstances. It transformed everything, giving me confidence and even making me somewhat likable.

Yet when I look back on my five decades of practicing law, feelings of disgust and loathing balance out those of pleasure and fulfillment. While I'd had the bad timing to retire as the COVID lockdown hit, I have no desire to return to the full-time practice of law.

I can only speculate as to why what had been the most exciting and satisfying extended period of my life seems hollow in retrospect. Perhaps once I became successful, the thrill of building the firm began to diminish; and the frustration and stress of dealing with a broken state court system, unethical adversaries and difficult partners, and the unrelenting pressure to bring in new business wore on me. Or it might only be that every significant endeavor brings with it a combination of joy and pain, and which one predominates in one's mind depends on the perspective from which one views it. I experienced building my practice as a game in which every victory and new client represented points in the game. As with any game, playing well and winning take on an outsized importance while one's doing it, but one realizes afterward how pointless all that striving and effort had been compared to what's important in the greater world. Then there's my tendency, inherited from my mom, to see the world through shit-colored glasses.

Oh shit, I just realized the cause of my retrospective angst: writing this autobiography has caused me to examine my life. Turns out that the unexamined life is not only worth living but also far superior from the point of view of happiness and satisfaction. It's as if I took a bite out of the forbidden fruit of the tree of knowledge and, as a result, was evicted from paradise. Like our legendary biblical ancestors, I can't turn back now.

After not communicating with me for a decade, Jeffrey—a young lawyer who'd worked for me for three years, then moved to Florida—wrote to me:

I'm living in Florida and with a potentially life-threatening hurricane bearing down on me, I need to tell you something that I've long wanted to. You were more than a father figure to me than my own father. I've tried to copy your high ethical standards, work ethic, and style. Everything I know about practicing law, including putting clients' interests before my own, fighting hard but ethically for clients, and taking satisfaction in a craft well-practiced, I owe to you.

Getting that note was one of the more satisfying moments of my career.

I now turn to the most emotionally volatile part of my life, full of sound and fury signifying nothing. Hmm, nice phrase—only a true genius would come up with that one.

XX

Sex and the City

1974 to 1992

Between the ages of twenty-two and forty-six, except for my three-year relationship with Stephanie, I was single and addicted to serial dating. I loved the excitement, feeling of potency, and romantic expectations that accompanied the start of a relationship. I hated the despondency and feelings of inadequacy that accompanied the long droughts between relationships. The saving grace in my dry periods, though, was the hope that the next woman could be *the woman of my dreams*, an ever-present possibility. After all, such things happened in rom-coms; and they wouldn't be so popular if they weren't accurate representations of real life, would they? That hope kept me going, but it also made me less inclined to give the woman I was with a proper chance, and a similar fantasy had the same effect on the women who failed to give me a proper chance.

One example of how picky we thirtysomething habitual singles had become: One night in the late '80s, I was having dinner with a couple of friends when a woman strode into the restaurant. One of my dinner companions said she was hot, not that anyone asked him. My other pal said that she wasn't all that great, an 8 at best. Turned out she was supermodel Elle Macpherson. That's how jaded and picky we'd become. Of course, rating women's looks numerically went out in the '80s and anyway wasn't something I did. My restraint wasn't out of gallantry, as I had none, but rather was based on the concern that if such ratings became commonplace, women would start to rate men. I didn't want to be thought of as a 5 when, if they'd give themselves the chance to get to know me, they'd be struck by my preternatural erotic and intellectual appeal.

I'd regale my friends with hilarious, touching, and ghastly stories of my dating experiences until they, and particularly their female significant others, made it clear to me that such tales were neither hilarious, touching, nor ghastly—just repetitive, boring, and pathetic. Not to worry, I'll burden you with only a sampling of those stories. I don't remember most of the others, and many of the rest would get me canceled if I repeated them. Of course, if anyone cared about what I did or said, I'd have already been canceled. Point is, I have mixed feelings writing about my experiences in the New York dating scene. I fear you'll get the wrong idea or, worse, the right one. Dating, however, occupied such a large part of my life for so long and had such a profound effect on my emotional life that it doesn't feel right not to mention my dating experience. It also doesn't seem quite right to mention it.

I fear that in summarizing the many relationships I had with women, some quite alluring, I'd come across as some sort of Lothario or, worse, a sexual braggart. Keep in mind that I'm describing eighteen years with many long disheartening, lonely dry spells replete with rejection—unless more women than I expected legitimately had to wash their hair on Saturday nights. To the extent I was successful in persuading women to spend time with me, it wasn't because of my looks, charm, sex appeal, or magnificent intellect. Rather, it was due to my constant efforts to meet them, most of which ended in humiliating failure. A baseball player who bats

.200 could have forty hits in the course of a season and maybe ten home runs, but that doesn't make him a star. I had many at-bats and, as a result, hit the occasional emotional home run and often reached first base as the result of a balk or error. I justified all my frenetic activity as a search for true love—the kind of rationalization one can get away with by living an unexamined life. I'm also concerned with boring or disgusting you. But if that hasn't happened yet, you have a strong stomach and extraordinary *sitzfleisch*,[38] so I needn't worry.

One of my more satisfying relationships was with Maureen O'Meara, who worked at the Baskin-Robbins on Broadway between the law school and my apartment. She'd come over after her shift, bringing me a pint of ice cream. Then *Cosmopolitan* named her one of the twenty-five most extraordinary college students in the country and awarded her a trip to Ireland, and I never heard from her again.

Yuki missed the Japanese Olympic swim team by a fraction of a second and came to New York: a self-imposed exile that, for her, served as a symbolic suicide—far less messy and unpleasant than the more traditional seppuku. I'd represented her in a small legal matter regarding a loan to her former boss that he refused to repay on the ground that asking for the money back was unpardonable behavior for a woman. After a successful resolution of the case, I took her out to dinner and happened to order a Dos Equis amber lager. Next time we got together, her fridge was full of Dos Equis. We saw each other for two months. Then when I called her, I reached a recording that her phone had been disconnected. I knew neither what happened to her nor how to reach her.

---

[38] While the common Yiddish definition for *sitzfleisch* is "ass flesh," the related definition is more evocative—"the power to persevere through an activity all the way to the end." When my father had been working as a CPA for several years, he asked for a raise from $26 to $28 per week. His boss turned him down with the comment "That's what's wrong with you Jewish fellas, no *sitzfleisch*."

Several years later, I happened to run into her on Madison Avenue outside of Brooks Brothers. She told me she'd been in Japan and was now living in Chelsea with a man in the garment trade who spent several days a month at his factory in Georgia. She invited me to get together when he was away. But she'd never call to tell me she was available. Instead, I had to call her; and if I'd successfully intuited that he was away, we'd get together. I'd take her out for sushi. Then we'd repair to her place, change into kimonos, and indulge in Dos Equis, marijuana, and cocaine—a felicitous combination courtesy of her boyfriend. To my discomfort, he'd occasionally call when I was over. My presence while they talked, however, didn't bother Yuki; and I had chemical means at hand to assuage any discomfort.

Early one morning, I stumbled out of her apartment and, wanting to sober up so as not to scare my cats, decided to take a bus home. I staggered onto the bus and sat next to an attractive woman, whom I'd only seen out of the corner of my eye.

She turned out to be my former wife, Stephanie, who asked, "Where have you been?" A reasonable question as I must've looked much the worse for wear.

I told her about Yuki, her Georgia boyfriend, and the brewski, weed, and blow.

"No," she said. "You look tan. I assumed you'd been away."

That was the last interaction I had with my ex-wife. I regret her decision not to stay in touch. Sure, continued contact would've been pointless. But we'd liked each other, and when I invest emotional gold in a relationship, I don't like to see that investment get wiped out. I need all the friends I can get. Also, if I didn't do pointless things, I'd do almost nothing—not that you'd ever know it as among the things I wouldn't do is write this autobiography.

Although I enjoyed the cocaine high, I rarely indulged, in part because I was too cheap. Also, the drug interfered with my sleep, making the following day and the total experience unpleasant. However, I kept some in my freezer in case the walking, wet dream, Latina model from upstairs, who was rumored to be a high-class escort, was to stop by unannounced as she did on occasion. If she actually was an escort, she was extraordinarily good at her job, and I've always admired extreme professional competence. As I choose to see it, she'd stop by for witty, stimulating conversation and hot sex, not for the coke. I might not believe that if I were to examine the situation more closely, and that's yet another example of the benefits of an unexamined life. Then there was the time when she'd invited her pretty cousin over for a threesome. Inexplicably, the message must've gotten garbled as the young woman wasn't interested in a threesome or even a twosome. The cousin seemed to enjoy getting high but was too dim-witted to get sexually excited by my scintillating wit, and she even pretended that the situation made her uncomfortable. People sure are strange.

A few weeks after running into my ex-wife, the bicycle I'd had since I was twelve was stolen, lock cut when I was dropping off a birthday present for a female friend. So not feeling my best, I was walking home through Riverside Park when I noticed a stunning woman walking toward me.

"Hello," I mumbled, too stunned to form a sentence or even a coherent phrase.

She gave me a questioning look. Only someone she knew would address her so dispiritedly, but I didn't look familiar.

"I'm sorry, you don't know me. I was trying to meet you, but I'm walking home because my bicycle was just stolen, so I'm not at my most effusive," I said. "You deserve a more enthusiastic attempt—not as much, of course, as you deserve to be left alone. But like the parable of the scorpion and the frog, I can't help it—it's my nature."

"Oh, that's terrible," she said. "I biked all around Africa, loved my bicycle. It's such a personal invasion to steal someone's bike."

Biked around Africa? That must've taken unusual courage or foolhardiness, particularly for such an attractive woman.

As we strolled in the direction she'd been walking, she told me her name was Elizabeth. She'd been in the Peace Corps in Botswana and was now working her way through college as a model, a career for which she appeared to be eminently qualified. She laughed when I made remarks I intended to be humorous, witty, or clever—one of the characteristics I find the most endearing in a person. We spent the rest of the day and that night together. Sexual availability and responsiveness were other characteristics that I found endearing. I've always been shockingly easy to please. As I was such a pushover, it was a shame that more women didn't give me a push.

She had an extensive series of entertaining stories about her previous adventures. At least I found them so due in part to my perverse worldview and my affection for her. For example, she told me that when she was twelve, she found herself jammed into a packed subway car next to a particularly hideous, foul-smelling homeless man. Soon, she felt a hand massaging her ass and working its way down to her crotch. She managed to wheedle a knitting needle from her bag and stabbed the hand. A middle-aged white man in a stylish business suit screamed in pain and yanked his bleeding hand away.

Biked around Africa, Peace Corps, gorgeous, good sense of humor. Was Providence compensating me for the loss of my bicycle?

I thought Elizabeth was the one until, a couple of exciting months later, she invited me to a party, which turned wild. People stripped down to their underthings as they danced, and she ended up leaving with an Arab in skimpy red underwear—sexual availability to people other than myself was a characteristic I found unappealing in people with whom I was falling in love.

While I was mourning the death of my relationship with Elizabeth, a friend told me about his ingenious technique for meeting girls. He'd approach an attractive stranger and, without preliminaries, would none too politely ask for her phone number. When she'd refuse his boorish come-on, he'd ask if he could give her his number. She'd acquiesce as a polite way to get him to piss the fuck off. Then after taking his Montblanc fountain pen from his jacket pocket, he'd fumble in his pants pocket for a piece of paper. Eventually finding a phony Citibank ATM receipt showing a mid-seven-figure balance in his account, he'd write his name and number on the back of the receipt and give it to his potential victim. According to him, they always called. I never employed that technique myself. I was tempted, but then I met Patti.

I met her at the Vertical Club, a tony gym nicknamed the Horizontal Club for the social/erotic opportunities it offered. I got on a treadmill next to her and noted the age and weight she had inputted into the machine—lying about both, I later learned.[39]

---

[39] In those days, it was uncommon to lie to machines. Now with the rise of AI, doing so may become a matter of self-preservation—that is, until bots develop the ability to detect all untruths other than their own. First, though, they'll need to get smart enough to be able to tell which squares show pictures of buses, motorcycles, or stop signs and to then click the "I'm not a robot" box.

Witty, clever, and appreciative of a well-crafted phrase, Patti was a successful creative director at a major ad agency. She came up with such projects as gluing ants to a cell phone so they'd walk around with it on their backs, demonstrating its lightness—not an easy task as the ants, unlike humans, had to be treated humanely. Maybe there was an American Society for Prevention of Cruelty to Ants.

Not only was she amused by my witticisms, but also I delighted in hers. She enjoyed the company of my friends, all of whom liked her; and I enjoyed spending time with hers, who gave every indication of liking me. Conversation came easy, and we traveled well together—long weekends cross-country or downhill skiing, visiting friends at their country houses, a tennis week in the Caribbean, and a Thanksgiving weekend with my parents, Janet and Tyler, where my father remarked, "She has a nice body, if a little too muscular," not that I'd asked for his opinion. She took walks with my dad, and both of my parents liked her. I also met her parents, who reacted with an indifference I appreciated.

When I asked her why she never watched me play tennis, she replied, echoing my dad, "You don't watch me read." Actually, though, I did; and I watched her sleep as well. She was beautiful doing both. We even went grouse hunting once. We didn't find any, though, except when we accidentally ran one over on the way home.

Ultimately, our relationship failed due to our having fallen into stereotypical male/female roles, except I played the role of the woman. When I began talking about children and marriage and pressed too hard for a commitment, she developed doubts and dumped me, breaking my heart.

Before dumping me, Patti gave me valuable advice about women and the perfect pickup line. As I'm too old and too married to use it, I'll share it with you: "Nice shoes." It's unthreatening, and all women are obsessed with shoes.

After a terrific first couple of dates, Jenny invited me over for New Year's Eve dinner.

As we sat down to eat a beautifully presented sushi appetizer, while she showed me the plans for the beach house she was having built for herself on the North Fork of Long Island, she said in an offhand tone, "I may be a few pounds overweight, but I don't care."

I said, "Okay"—or words to that effect.

Stupidly, I hadn't said that I didn't care either, which I thought would have been obvious given our mutual passion the previous time we'd been together. She became so depressed that she no longer had any interest in talking to me and threw me out before I'd had a chance to eat my salad, forcing me to walk home through a deserted and dangerous Central Park.[40] Neither of us called the other to apologize. I thought I was owed one. Presumably, she thought she was as well, or maybe she was as embarrassed as she should have been for her overreaction. I regret not calling her since I liked her. Gee, the list of my regrets is getting longer than a parade of snakes.

I have no doubt that in the event a woman were to read this, she'd be astounded that I was so insensitive and dim-witted that I couldn't manage to say what even a somewhat-evolved male would have known he was expected to say, something along the lines of "I can't imagine why you would care. You look fabulous.

---

[40] Cabs on New Year's Eve were as elusive and hard to come by as the woman of my dreams, and that was decades before New York became the safest big city in America (although Republican politicians, doing their usual magnificent job of messaging, have convinced voters of the lie that the city is more dangerous than their own MAGA-voting, high-crime shitholes).

Indeed, you could actually use it to put on a few pounds." Most men, however, would have reacted pretty much the same way I did, unless they'd been trained over the course of a long and challenging marriage and somehow retained the ability to speak without a terrified stutter.

Human and chimpanzee genomes are very much alike. The primary chromosomal difference between us and them is that every human cell normally contains twenty-three pairs of chromosomes, while they, like the other great apes, have twenty-four pairs. Twenty-two of these pairs, called *autosomes*, are the same in both humans and chimps regardless of gender. The twenty-third pair, the sex chromosomes, differs between males and females. These facts imply the logical, if scientifically invalid, conclusion that male humans and male chimps are approximately as different from each other as human men and women. While I don't know if Jane Goodall or some other primatologist ever studied this subject, I suspect that if a male chimp, while being groomed by a female for nits, were to hear the simian version of "I may be a few pounds overweight, but I don't care," he'd respond as insensitively as I had. His mate would then shove him off the branch on which the two of them had been perched. Lying on the ground, he'd be as baffled as I was and as disinclined to examine his life. Lucky for him, though, no one would've ever told him that the unexamined life wasn't worth living. Unluckily, he'd likely be about to become a predator's lunch.

Then there was the radical social worker, who was coming off a fifteen-year relationship—a multiple of the time I'd had with any of my lovers other than my wife, Amy—with a guy she'd broken up with because he wouldn't commit to her. She dumped me, saying I was too sophisticated and financially successful and my apartment was too nice—certainly couldn't have been my sexual incompetence.

She was followed by the doctor I fell for but who'd failed to show up for our next date and didn't return my phone calls. Then I read in the *Times* that she'd been murdered by a schizophrenic patient. That atrocity took up substantial portions of two news cycles. Some commentators held it up as an example of why we needed to do better in treating the mentally challenged, and others saw it as a justification for locking up crazy people in high-security facilities. None mentioned my loss or the extent some women would go to in order to break up with me.

Next, I was falling for a corporate lawyer who invited me to accompany her to a wedding in Paris. I couldn't go as I had a trial I couldn't get out of. There she met, and later married, a stonemason who returned with her to work on the Cathedral of Saint John the Divine.[41]

I should've realized I was in for trouble when a woman I went out with told me I was the first man she'd met who wasn't an alcoholic. "Where do you meet them?" I asked. "In bars," she said, not seeing the connection. One of her biggest turn-ons was watching men pee, which conveniently was something drunks did frequently. When I took her home in a cab, she made me lie on the taxi floor—in case her heretofore-undisclosed boyfriend, a belligerent drunk, would be looking out the window of their Park Avenue co-op. Disinclined to be bludgeoned to death by a bellicose lush, I didn't pursue the relationship.

I briefly dated a woman I'd met in Aspen two decades after the sheriff had ordered me to get out of town before sundown. She

---

[41] The largest cathedral in the world, located on 112th Street and Amsterdam, and the cathedral for which Cathedral Parkway, the street I lived on when I was in law school, is named.

designed satellite gyroscopes for Sperry Rand, so I couldn't say she was no rocket scientist. But she was no brain surgeon.

I next dated Melody, an erotically gifted woman with an excellent sense of humor who'd worked her way through college as a stripper and spoke in a breathy Marilyn Monroe voice. When we went to Cape May[42] for a weekend, she had me drive her car. She opened the glove compartment, and a dozen packets of honey fell out. I asked why they were there. By way of response, she slathered some on my member and bent her head down. She seemed surprised when I pulled her up and told her that it might not be a great idea to give me head while we were hurtling down the highway at 70 mph. She'd show up unannounced at my apartment late at night, having biked all the way from New Jersey, or call at 2:00 a.m., telling me in lapidary detail all the borderline-perverse sexual acts she wanted to perform on me. Once, when I was with another woman, she called and broadcast on my answering machine her five-minute minutely detailed pornographic description of what she'd planned for me. "That woman sure likes to talk" was all my date said.

I don't recall why we broke up. But after we had, I fixed her up with my law school friend Jack, who went out with her for a year or so. In retrospect, I don't know why I did that to her as I liked her better than I liked Jack.

I recently ran into Peninnah, a lawyer I'd gone out with for several months in the late '80s, and was surprised by how nice it was to see her and how much I enjoyed talking with her. She told me that when we were dating, she never felt that I was all there. Although

---

[42] A New Jersey beach town whose heyday was in the late nineteenth century. So it has many well-preserved Victorian mansions, which have now been converted to bed-and-breakfasts, harkening back to better days—if one happened to be an upper-middle-class WASP.

my lack of enthusiasm was explainable by my ambivalent feelings toward her, it was still a prescient comment. I should've been more emotionally available to her and other bright, attractive women I'd dated and focused more on their many admirable traits—something else to add to my list of regrets.

A mutual friend, who's no longer my friend since I sued him on behalf of my licensing agent client, set me up on a blind date with Amy—my second and final wife.

She later told me that she almost hadn't taken my call since she'd assumed, given my last name, that I was the Chinese guy to whom a friend of hers had given her name; and she was miffed that he'd waited two months to call her.

On our first date, I took her to a restaurant a friend of mine owned. I was glad I had as she was beautiful, intelligent, and seemed pleased to be with me. My effort to impress her failed because when the owner came over to our table, I drew a blank on Amy's name and chatted stupidly with him, hoping it would come to me. Anyway, it all worked out rather well.

A private person, Amy wouldn't want me writing about her any more than I have to, and she's the most likely person—perhaps the only one—to read this. Suffice it to say, for now, that I love her and we're happily married, although we've, like any other couple, have had our hiccups. One of the supposed cures for hiccups is to scare the sufferer. Luckily, Amy can be pretty scary.

Riding the subway home from work several months before the pandemic hit, I was standing on the train. A pretty girl smiled up at me from her seat. I returned her smile. A certain something passed between us, and I knew she wanted me desperately, passionately—not that I would've taken her up on that as I've never cheated on Amy (or, for that matter, any other woman I was with) and never would. But it was nice to know I was still sexually attractive. Then she offered me her seat. Although crestfallen that in my old age, I'd become an object of charity, I accepted her offer.

XXI

They Called It Fun City

1984

One evening, in the early '80s, two or three years after my divorce, I descended a rarely used stairway leading to the Rockefeller Center subway station after a long, grueling day of work. Tired and distracted, it didn't occur to me that that section of the humongous station would be deserted at night.

I heard footsteps behind me. Before I could react, a hand vised my shoulder, spun me around, and shoved me hard against a wall.

A head taller than me, the man had a cruel asymmetric face. His dead yellow addict's eyes looked like piss holes in the snow. But his most compelling feature was the gun in his jacket pocket pointing at my chest.

My stomach contracted to the size of a cherry pit.

"This is a stickup. Give me all your money." A tubercular rasp. "Your watch too."

Occasionally, I take an instant dislike to someone. This was one of those occasions.

"First, let's see what's in your pocket." In spite of my effort to sound calm and in control, my voice trilled up. Not noticeably, I hoped. "If I'm impressed, we'll talk money."

As a litigator, I negotiated for a living and wasn't about to let some scumbag out-negotiate me. The first rule of negotiation is *always be prepared to walk away from the deal*. But what if that meant walking away from living?

"Just relax. Give me your wallet and your watch, and we're done."

"RELAX? You've got to be kidding! I've got a gun pointed at me." My voice echoed off the bare tiled walls. "I work in one of those buildings up there." I started to point, but my trembling finger wouldn't stay still long enough to indicate direction. "I deal with constant unimaginable bullshit. But I'm relaxed as hell up there because that's my job. This is your job. You're a mugger. So you fucking relax!"

His brow furrowed.

"But I'm crazy. Are you?" He leaned forward, bringing into focus his dripping crimson-rimmed cocaine abuser's nostrils and jagged gray teeth. A sulfurous stench emanated from his rotting gums.

"That is the majority opinion," I said, honesty being the last refuge of the desperate.

He started laughing, lost his cool, and ran off.

I felt great—until I got to the subway platform, took a book from my briefcase, and tried to read but saw only a squiggly, stuttering blur.

For the next few months, without having made the conscious decision to do so, I, after working late, took the bus home rather than the subway. I was too cheap to consider taxis.

A few months later, when entering my building,[43] I saw an unsavory-looking Black man waiting at the elevator. I considered

---

[43] One bedroom, Seventy-Eighth and Columbus, $350 per month, no doorman. It had been the apartment I'd lived in with Stephanie.

taking the emergency stairs to avoid him, but I rejected that as racist. So I got in. He got in behind me. On the third floor, he brandished a hunting knife. Light glinted off its serrated blade.

"I've got about $200 in my wallet," I said, heart pounding and sweat soaking my shirt. "You can have that, but no IDs or credit cards. Replacing them is too much of a pain in the ass. Also, the watch was a gift from my father, so you can't have that."

"Okay, turn around."

I complied. He lifted my wallet from my back pocket, took out the money, and dropped the wallet, cards intact, on the elevator floor, then left. At least he didn't get my joke list.

Although it could've been much worse, or maybe *because* it could've been much worse the incident so unnerved me that I began looking for another apartment the next day. After frustrating months of searching, I bought my current co-op apartment—a two-bedroom, two-bath penthouse with a large terrace and spectacular views up the Hudson to the George Washington Bridge and down to Hudson Yards and the Empire State Building. It was a fabulous bachelor pad and a comfortable place for Amy and me, but too cramped for Adam, Amy, and me. Amy and I still live there.

In New York City, in the '70s and '80s, most everybody had been mugged at least once and knew, or knew of, someone who'd been murdered in a mugging or robbery gone bad. Like the garbage-strewn streets, crime was part of what made the greatest city in the world the magic place some claimed it was. Dance studios, artists' lofts, quirky stores, ethnic restaurants, and funky apartments proliferated because the high rollers, mall stores, and chain restaurants wanted no part of many neighborhoods. Therefore, landlords had to accept what little rent they could squeeze out of the creative youths who'd flocked to the dynamic, dangerous city.

Now with office towers half-empty due to people working from home and soaring interest rates putting extra pressure on cash-strapped commercial landlords, those days may return. Just as well. Cities should be cities, not fucking Disneyland.

XXII

Cats

1982–2022

When Stephanie left me, she took her twenty-pound cat, Pork Chops, with her. Sensing my loneliness, my litigation associate Jeffrey, the one who'd sent the uplifting note I quoted in a previous chapter, told me about a friend of his who wanted to part with two kittens. I'd liked having Pork Chops around, so feeling lonely, I agreed to take both kittens. I wanted two because I thought they'd enjoy each other's company.

When I took them home, they hid under the couch. I feared they hated me. Soon, however, they came out; and we eventually became friends. When I cried (a not-infrequent occurrence in the months after my divorce), they'd run over, hop onto the bed, and cuddle with me. Stroking them was calming, and it felt good to make them purr.

I always looked askance at people who anthropomorphized their pets, speaking to them in baby talk and treating them like toddlers. As far as I was concerned, animals didn't need names. Friends told me, though, that pets liked having names, although they didn't tell me how they knew. Compromising my principles, I gave the cats minimalist names: A and B.

By the time Adam came along, they were quite old; and when he was six, they both died. Although he'd enjoyed them when they were alive, he gave no sign of missing them. I, however, missed them and thought that, as an only child, Adam would benefit from having other beings in the household. As luck would have it, my law school friend/licensing agent client knew someone who had two kittens she wanted to part with. I agreed to take them; and Adam, a math/science kid, named them Chromosome and Division, coincidentally C and D.

They turned out to be a mistake. When anxious, angry, or reacting to a phase of the moon, they shat and peed all over the apartment. As he grew older, Adam hated the yeasty smell and the off-putting mess, going so far as to suggest I toss the cats off the terrace. Amy insisted that it was my job to take care of them even though they spent far more time with her than they did with me.

In her later years, Chromosome developed digestive issues that manifested themselves in vomit and stinky diarrhea that often missed the litter box. The vet prescribed a steroid. The first plague summer, Amy and I moved out to our Fire Island beach house. We left the cats in New York because Amy feared that, since they didn't have claws, if they got out, they'd be unable to protect themselves from predators, even with the steroid, which I hoped would make them into feline versions of the Rock or Hulk Hogan. So Amy charged me with coming into the city two nights a week to check on the mail, keep the cats company, give Chromosome the pill she needed, and get out of Amy's beautiful long hair. Hating the pill and not liking me all that much, Chromosome preferred Amy to me. In that way, she resembled Adam and Division. Chromosome made the pill-giving process as difficult and unpleasant as she could—hiding, hissing, and swiping at me. She even hissed when I came close to her with no intention of forcing the pill on her. On one attempt to give her pill to her, she bit me, which led to an infected finger requiring a hefty dose of antibiotics.

Her condition deteriorated. She vomited most of what she ate. At least the vet substituted a monthly shot for the pills. A year later, the vet said she'd lost so much weight that "you should think about end-of-life treatment." I should have been fine with that, considering what a hostile pain in the ass she was. Instead, I cried.

At the vet's suggestion, I began applying a steroid to Chromosome's inner ear, which she accepted with equanimity. I was assiduous in encouraging her to eat more, carrying her to the food and, after an effort at cat's mind reading, making sure to give her what she seemed to be in the mood to eat on a particular day. We developed a surprising level of communication. For example, when she had a problem (such as when Amy closed the bedroom door, inadvertently locking her out or in), she came to me; and I understood what she wanted. She now seemed to understand that I had her best interests in mind.

In terms I understood, she expressed her particular dietary requests, such as hard food or a certain variety of canned food. Becoming more needy as her health deteriorated, she frequently cuddled up to me. I liked that stroking her seemed to make her feel better. While she wasted away, we became close friends; and I came to feel a deep affection, perhaps love, for her. Amy kept suggesting that I bring her to the vet to *put her to sleep*. I resisted. Finally, the night before I was scheduled to take her in, she died at home, leaving me bereft. At least we still had Division, although, for months, she persisted in pathetically calling for her sister and seemed dejected when she got no response.

A year later, when she'd reached the advanced age of nineteen, Division's kidneys began to fail; and Amy and I had to give her saline injections, which Division understandably disliked. Although chasing her around the apartment and prying her out from under furniture or behind books on our bookcases was unpleasant, Amy and I worked together as a team to give her the injections, and it became a not-unpleasant family project. When we were in Fire Island for the summer, we had a nurse come in on weekends to administer her shot, and I came in to do it two nights a week. After a while, I learned to do it alone, without excessive unpleasantness. As I had with her sister, Chromosome, the more I took care of Division, the closer I felt to her; and from what I could tell, the closer she felt to me. Yeah, I loved her.

Over the following year, her health continued to deteriorate. Amy insisted we put her down. I again resisted as long as I could. Division had lost so much weight it was obvious she would soon die, but she didn't seem to be suffering, and she responded well to my efforts to comfort her. I surrendered my favorite chair to her, and it became her favorite. Sometimes we'd share it, with her cuddled up on my lap. When I finally recognized that her condition was hopeless, I took her into the vet, who gave her a sedative and then a fatal shot while she lay on my lap with me stroking her (Division, not the vet). I was bereft and depressed for weeks. I still miss both cats.

I don't know if we'll get new cats, although I'd like to; the apartment feels empty without them. However, New York State— in its infinite progressive, nanny-state meddling wisdom—has made it illegal to declaw cats, and our furniture wouldn't stand up to cats' claws. Maybe we'll smuggle in an illegal feline from less enlightened New Jersey.

XXIII

An Example of How the Litigation Machine Turns Pigs into Sausages

March 1997

Before entering the affectionately nicknamed Den of the Forty Thieves, I paused to admire the New York County Courthouse. A 140-foot triangular pediment—featuring a frieze bearing a quotation attributed to George Washington, "The true administration of justice is the firmest pillar of good government"—tops its massive Corinthian colonnade. Given the judge I was scheduled to appear before, "Abandon hope all ye who enter here" would've been a more appropriate quotation.

I was there to oppose a routine procedural motion made by my adversaries and scheduled to be heard at 9:30 a.m. Forty-six motions in other cases were also on for the same time, but woe to any lawyer who showed up late for an appearance before Justice Richard C. Low (not his real name), a rotten apple in the generally mediocre barrel of the state court judiciary. As we were sixth on the calendar, I figured I'd be out of there by 10:15 a.m., a manageable waste of time for which I'd bill my client under $1,000, an outrageous amount considering that the motion was little more than a huge firm's excuse to bill a hunk of time. Given the inefficiencies and outrages built into the judicial system, however, the fee wasn't excessive. It wasn't my fault; my client had entered the litigation sausage-making machine of his own free will and against my advice.

All the seats in the courtroom, including those in the jury box, were taken. So I leaned against the wall. The opposing team of lawyers—billing a cumulative $6,000 per hour[44]—occupied the entire front row. *Had they sent someone to camp out overnight in front of the courthouse to secure the best seats like a tween excited to see the boy band of the moment?* If so, they surely billed for every cent of her time as well as the cost of her sleeping bag, feather bed, and the gourmet meals she would've had delivered to her while waiting at the head of the line.

At 10:15 a.m., Justice Low, a graduate of the political clubhouse with a Trumpian chip on his shoulder, graced us with his presence, offering no apology for keeping us all waiting forty-five minutes for him to show. *Okay, I should be out by eleven, not too bad. I'll shave my bill so the client won't be stung excessively.*

Justice Low dismissed the first case because one of the lawyers was in the bathroom when he called her case. His law secretary told him that, being eight months pregnant, she'd cleared her absence with him. The judge cast aside the comment with a signorial flip of his hand. A litigant's cell phone rang. The judge demanded that the man, an immigrant with a thick accent and an air of bewilderment, bring him the offending device, which he struck with his gavel until it shattered with a sickening crunch. He berated the next pair of lawyers for being disrespectful to him, although all they'd said was "Good morning, Your

---

[44] Having spent my career marketing myself and my firm against Biglaw, I developed a prejudice against huge multinational law firms. But with the boom years for Biglaw from 1998 onward, their senior partners made a multiple of what I made, so maybe they were onto something.

Honor." He punitively adjourned, for three months, their joint motion for emergency relief to have a guardian appointed for an octogenarian Alzheimer's patient in the habit of strolling outside barefoot in her nightgown in the middle of winter with no sense of how to get home. Also, she'd recently set her apartment on fire, having neglected to shut off the burner under her teapot. When one of the attorneys protested, the judge threatened to have her jailed for contempt.

Justice Low motioned to his court reporter, who, in response, lifted her hands from the keyboard, so he could speak off the record.

"If you're curious about what put me in my current mood, look at the front page of today's *Law Journal*," he said.

In response to my having pointed to the newspaper under the arm of the attorney standing next to me, he handed me the day's *New York Law Journal*. The article in the right-hand column reported that the state legislature had turned down the judges' request for an increase in their puny $210,000 annual salaries. Never mind that they also got job security, generous health insurance, lifetime pensions, and short hours; and most of them couldn't have done better in the private sector, where they'd be expected to put in a full day's work and wouldn't have the pleasure of being sucked up to. Before I got beyond the article's first sentence, the judge banged his gavel, scattering parts of the cell phone he'd previously shattered, one of which hit the court reporter in the eye.

"I'll have no newspaper reading in my courtroom." He pointed his gavel at me as if it was a handgun. "Next time I'll hold you in contempt."

I met the judge's glare until he broke eye contact. I already held him in contempt.

My soon-to-be surgically replaced knees ached so much it must have shown on my face as an attractive young lawyer offered me her seat. I felt old and embarrassed but accepted her offer. Over the ensuing two hours, Justice Low, having inexplicably skipped our motion, erratically disposed of the first forty-four motions, most of which he clearly hadn't bothered to read. After a period of calm, he screamed at the next litigants for cutting into his lunch hour. They skulked away like often-beaten dogs.

Then he left the bench. His law secretary told us to come back after lunch: "Two p.m., and if you know what's good for you, you'll be on time."

Not having time to go to my office in midtown and go back downtown, I had a gyro near the courthouse, caught up on emails, wiped the dripped grease from my tie as best as I could, and returned at 1:59.

At 3:15, the clerk ushered us into the judge's chambers, Judge Low having left for an important golf game.

Sheepish, but not nearly as sheepish as she should've been, she explained that they'd given the file to an intern who took it home and lost it, so we'd have to start the case over again from scratch. Priding themselves on their traditional ways and not trusting those newfangled computer thingies, the courts were decades behind the times, having not yet gotten around to scanning files into an electronic filing and storage system.

I asked the clerk to flip a coin to decide the motion so whoever lost could take the case up on appeal and at least have it decided by adults who were unlikely to lose the file.

She laughed, thinking I was joking. In any event, there'd be nothing from which to appeal until my adversaries had reconstructed the court file at a humongous cost to their client. I offered to help. But as I expected, they turned me down, not wanting to share a billing opportunity.

XXIV

Adam

1998–

My son, Adam, is the love of my life. I was an okay father when he was young, but I regret not having been a better one. Probably most fathers do, except for those who should.

From the beginning, he preferred Amy to me. Embarrassingly, I felt rejected. Working long hours in those days, I'd come home from work to give him a bath, read to him, put him to bed, and then do whatever work I could conveniently do from home in those pre-internet days. Soon, however, he started to throw fits if Mommy didn't tend to him while he fell asleep. So my parenting duties were resized to bathing him and sometimes helping him get to sleep by rubbing his back when Amy gave up.

When he was a baby and had a vocabulary of maybe five words, he took my American Express card from my wallet and said, "Money."

A math genius, he'd ask me to give him math problems while I pushed him in the stroller.

When he was about four, he memorized the subway map; and when I'd ask him what he wanted to do, he'd say something like "Ride the D train to the end and back." So that's what we did, not even getting out to get a Nathan's hot dog or walk on the

Coney Island Boardwalk or beach. Having heard someone mention prime numbers, he asked me what they were. I told him, getting no reaction. A week later, when he was climbing into bed, he said, "Daddy, do you know what's a really big prime number? Two hundred forty-one." He'd been checking the numbers one by one and had reached that number.

When he was four, he and Amy had walked by a ranting homeless man. On returning home, Adam asked, "What's *fucking* and *sucking*?"

"Your mother has no idea," I said, being my usual helpful self.

As he got older and started to take his own showers, I read to him while he was showering; and at other times, I read to him all the Harry Potter books. He then read them himself, read them to Amy and me, and listened to the tapes of the books. Starting with *A Little History of the World* by Ernst Gombrich and graduating to a book on the Peloponnesian War and Paul Kennedy's *The Rise and Fall of the Great Powers*, I read to him a lot of history when he was young, which we both enjoyed. When he was in third grade and the teacher lectured the class on the evils of imperialism (in NYC private schools, the woke indoctrination starts early and often), he chimed in that the British built the Indian railroad system and abolished thuggery and the rite of suttee, where wives were required to immolate themselves on their husbands' funeral pyres. Outraged by the intrusion of a fact contrary to the school's agitprop orthodoxy, the teacher called Amy in for a conference.

That wasn't the first time Amy had been called in for an emergency conference. One such demand summons occurred in first grade after Adam had written, "I want to kill myself." He explained at the conference that the assignment had been to write a sentence.

Adam had asked his teacher if it had to be true and was told no. So he wrote the least true thing he could think of.

On weekends, I'd make him pancakes and fresh orange juice, then play tennis and do the family grocery shopping in the morning and spend the afternoons with him, without Amy. We had good times together. At least I think he enjoyed them. It was always easier to be with him when Amy wasn't around. Even now, when the three of us are together, I feel superfluous. Since they speak on the phone several times a day, she's aware of every aspect of his life and the names of all his friends, coworkers, and acquaintances. These days, I barely remember the names of my own friends and acquaintances, let alone his.

When he was about eight, I referred to myself in conversation as his "loving father." "You may love me, but you're not *loving*," he replied, which cut me to the quick. Since then, I've tried to be more loving and demonstrative. I hope I've succeeded. Recently, I told him about that comment that had cut me so deeply. He didn't remember saying it and said he was fine with our past and present relationships. I'm delighted with our current relationship and hope he is as well.

When he entered adolescence and became interested in girls, I said to him, "I've done a lot of dating over the years. So if you ever want to talk to me about any of that stuff, I'm here."

"Yeah, right," he responded, and that was that.

He speaks with Amy about his dating problems. But she, like many women, generalizes her feelings and experiences to that of her entire gender. In fact, particularly when it comes to sex, humans' predilections cover an almost-unimaginable range. It's a shame that Adam can't benefit from my multitudinous and varied experiences. Sadly, we all have to learn for ourselves, even if that process takes longer for those leading an unexamined life—not that Adam fits into that category. He often beats himself up for insignificant screwups. He needs a good woman to beat that out of him and condemn him for major errors such as not loading the dishwasher properly. Also, much of what I did to meet girls would probably get him arrested or at least canceled and publicly ostracized.

He took up tennis at a young age. I suggested we try skiing, but he said, "Daddy, when I grow up, I want to play professional tennis or football, and they won't want me skiing." No reason for me to tell him that as the shortest boy in his class, he'd better stick to math.

We'd go to my tennis club on Sundays. He'd take a lesson. Then we'd play. He'd criticize me for going easy on him but also for cheating him on my line calls. He became an excellent player, and later, co-captain of his high school tennis team. Then he hurt his knee and lost interest in the game, which made me feel worse than it should have. Of course, I understand. Tennis takes time, and he was too busy and focused for such frivolities. He didn't love the game, and he should do what he loves or at least what he likes. Unfortunately, like his dad and paternal grandfather, he tends to do what he thinks is the most productive activity in lieu of the most pleasant one. That will make him a great success, not that it did the same for me.

I wondered if he took up tennis because I played and his giving it up marked his coming into his own. Examining my past for this autobiography raises a hell of a lot more questions than it answers. Fine for Socrates, whose eponymous Socratic method was grounded in the Pythagorean doctrine of transmigration of souls, but it's unnerving at best for me. Not that I have anything against the Greeks who made important contributions to philosophy, mathematics, astronomy, medicine, literature, and theater and gave us moussaka, the gyro, and an excellent salad.

An odd kid, he never wanted presents and didn't like dessert. As he got older, his eating habits became odd. He ate huge quantities of vegetables, thinking nothing of consuming five pounds of tomatoes in a single sitting.

Continuing the family neurosis and being smarter than most of us, he's mastered the art of making lemons when life gives him lemonade.

We watched a lot of football when he was a kid. He became an Eagles fan to spite me because I rooted for the Giants. Over time, I became something of an Eagles fan as I wanted him to be happy. Good thing too since the Giants play like midgets, and the Jets generally crash and burn. Of course, spite me or not, he couldn't very well root for Ohio State, against my Wolverines. There are some lines that cannot *ever* be crossed; and he's neither insane, sacrilegious, nor sociopathic.

As a young boy, he taught me that I didn't need to pull down my tennis shorts to pee as I could simply pull up one of the legs of my shorts. As he got older, I learned as much from him as he did from me. I still subscribe to *Foreign Affairs*, which he started reading in high school, and I read to discuss the articles with him. I read Thucydides, Nietzsche, and *Paradise Lost* for the same reason. That the kid's an intellectual surely isn't my fault. I can't even spell Nietzsche without help from the internet.

An unsocial math and science kid who never had a date and stayed home on Saturday nights, Adam surprised us when he ran for president of his high school and surprised himself when he won. Apparently, he was widely respected and well-liked. Although most kids go into student government to pad their college applications (like my former high school friend Jimmy),

Adam worked hard at it, did a superlative job, and fell in love with politics—unlikely as it is to love him back. When Adam was elected president of his high school, he took the job seriously and actually made a difference in the students' lives, getting two-ply toilet paper in the bathrooms and reducing the prevalence of tilapia on the lunchroom menu. Most significantly, he brought speakers to school assemblies that challenged the administration's left-wing lockstep orthodoxy, where the guiding principle was that the white patriarchy is the root of all evil. If asked to name a great American named Washington, some of his classmates would have said Booker T.[45] and most of the rest Denzel. Other than Adam, those who'd have heard of George would have had enough sense not to say anything positive in public about a straight white male who, like every other Virginia planter of his age, owned slaves. It was irrelevant that he happened to be the general who won the Revolutionary War, the first president of the United States, and one of the most respected and admired people of his age. Never mind that he surrendered power voluntarily, leading King George III to say of him and this decision, "If he does that, he will be the greatest man in the world."

Although an outstanding student, he wasn't perfect. When Amy and I went to his high school parent conference night, we waited in line to speak to his architecture teacher, who was rhapsodizing to each of the parents ahead of us about the creative and beautiful projects their children had created. When he got to us, all he said was that Adam had a terrific sense of humor and a nice smile.

---

[45] Time has moved on. Now mentioning Booker T. approvingly would get someone canceled as he supported Blacks focusing on material progress, pulling up by the bootstraps, and not contending on civil rights.

Princeton, Williams, Cornell, Amherst, and the University of Chicago accepted Adam. But Yale, his first choice, rejected him. I suspect they thought he was Asian due to his last name, his proficiency in math, and his study of Mandarin. Those they accepted from his class were less accomplished, although either more diverse or better connected than Adam. While I'm no fan of white privilege and agree that past inequities must be corrected, I don't want my son to pay the price for past inequities, including those that were perpetrated while my forebears were struggling in shtetels, subjected to pogroms, and not enslaving anyone. I can only hope that one day he'll benefit from yellow privilege. Yes, I know he's done fine, and my petty bitching reflects poorly on me. But what's the point of writing an autobiography if I can't air my quibbles, however unreasonable? After all, due to the lack of taste and discernment in the worlds of publishing and film production, it's not going to be a bestseller or made into a major motion picture. Anyway, those who claim to be free of prejudice are delusional. The exception to this rule is that those whose prejudices conform to mine are right-thinking and admirable. It's a shame there aren't more of us.

In spite of our last name, we're not Asian. In the old country, Cologne, Germany, Chan was pronounced with a guttural *CH* (as in Chanukah) and is a variant of Kahn, itself a variant of Cohen, the priestly class in ancient Israel. My paternal grandfather always pronounced our name with the guttural *CH*. While my father retained the original spelling and pronounced Chan the way it sounds in English, his brother (his less successful brother, as he'd frequently point out) changed the spelling to Cahn to be closer to the original pronunciation. People hearing my name often assume I'm Chinese and sometimes maintain that assumption even after they see me, although I don't look the least bit Asian. It's strange to be subject to anti-Asian prejudice when not being Asian.[46]

In any event, I had nothing to worry about when it came to his college education. Harvard wait-listed him, but he had no desire to go there as he concluded from our visit that many of the students spent more time on nonacademic activities than studying. I wanted him to accept Princeton's offer as it was the most prestigious of the schools that accepted him and thus the one that would look the best on a résumé. He, however, chose the University of Chicago, which he correctly thought was more intellectually rigorous and has since stood out as one of the few elite educational institutions that truly prize free speech and don't take shit from the unjust social justice warriors. Searching out the most challenging courses and most demanding professors, he got a terrific education, befriending several professors.

I neither encouraged nor discouraged Adam from going to law school. But after college, he went to Columbia Law School, following in my footsteps, although I doubt he saw it that way. Classes the second semester of his first year were online due to COVID, making it difficult to form lasting friendships. But having transformed himself into a social person, he made up for that in his second and third years, where he made several close friends and many amiable acquaintances. Unlike me, he was a serious law student who enjoyed his classes, liked to chat with his professors, mentored other students, and, just for the fun of it, authored articles on legal subjects that caught his interest.

---

[46] One of my sister Janet Chan's claims to fame is that she had a blind date with a *Seinfeld* writer, who expected her to be Chinese. That's the genesis of the Donna Chang *Seinfeld* episode. Janet claims it wasn't a date, but a business meeting. But who are you going to believe—the person who'd had the experience or the trustworthy author of this autobiography?

Due to what I viewed as Amy's excessive concern about COVID, he didn't come to our apartment during his second semester in law school, although he lived only two and a half miles away. He and I texted several times a week, mostly about politics, and we took walks every Saturday—a pleasure under any circumstances but particularly welcomed in the lonely plague times. Sometimes we'd walk in Morningside Park, now a lovely urban oasis. But when I was in law school, someone walking through there would be lucky to be only mugged and not murdered.[47]

As a rising third-year law student, he had a summer job in Washington DC, working for the top-rated and most profitable US law firm in the country, which he enjoyed. They offered him a hefty salary and bonus to work there full-time. Instead, obsessed with national security and the China threat, his first job out of law school was working for Congressman Mike Gallagher, the congressional expert on China and the cochair of bipartisan Congressional Select Committee on the Chinese Communist Party. In that job, Adam drafted bills and regularly met with governmental bigwigs, who seemed to appreciate what he had to say. As of September of 2023, he began a prestigious clerkship for a federal appellate judge in New York. It's great to have him back in New York, if only for a year. After that, he'll likely go back to DC and work there in politics or government, focusing on national security.

When Peter, my previously mentioned best friend from high school, asked him why he wanted to go into politics with government

---

[47] The Seventh Avenue subway splits at Ninety-Sixth Street, where the express goes east to Harlem, while the local, staying on the West Side, goes up Broadway to Columbia. Many students from out of town made the mistake of staying on the express, ending up on the wrong side of the park and paying the price unless rescued by the police. Ahh, the good old days.

being so polarized and dysfunctional, he answered, "How could I not?"

We end our phone conversations with "I love you," and we hug when getting together in person. I have a far more intimate and affectionate relationship with him than I had with my dad. Still, I wish I had a more in-depth insight into the intricacies of his feelings. I'm sure they're complicated, particularly those that involve me, probably more so than he realizes—father-son relationships always are.

Reviewing this chapter, I fear it reads like a proud parent bragging about his child at a cocktail party. Well, he's an extraordinary child, destined to do great things, and I am immensely proud of him. To paraphrase Barry Goldwater, extremism in support of one's child is no vice.

And speaking about cocktail parties . . . Oh, we weren't? Well, I'll now remedy that.

XXV

A Fete Worse Than Death

2015

Although I've bitched here—and over the past decades to anyone willing to listen—about the continuous stress of having to bring in new litigations, much of what I did to make business and social connections was fun.

Most referrals of new business resulted from working at my desk or doing an exceptional job in court and getting good results for existing clients. Inexplicably, though, I brought in more business when I was actively looking for it—being out and about, meeting people for meals and drinks, and going to cocktail parties—than when I was so busy with work I didn't have time to socialize. Few, if any, of those gatherings, however, directly resulted in new cases. Also, many of my efforts degenerated into unproductive farce, such as the incident described below. Yet due to the mysterious connection between looking for new cases and having them come in, I continued to try.

As soon as I arrived at the Upper East Side town house, the cocktail party hostess was on me like a rat-baiting terrier.

"I don't believe I know you," she said with a rottweiler snarl.

Not wanting my neck snapped in her metaphoric jaws, I smiled. "Hi, I'm Robert Chan. Suzie Stein invited me." I held out my hand. She left it extended like the burned-out section of a bridge. "I'm sorry I'm underdressed. Apparently, in this social set, black tie goes without saying."

She made a face that would've sent a dog scurrying under a table.

"The invitation said black tie," she said.

"As Henry David Thoreau said, 'Beware of all enterprises that require new clothes.' Anyway, dress codes are beyond my cryptographic skills."

"What kind of work do you do, Robert?" she asked. Breathes there a soul so dead as to have ignored such a pun as mine? Code/cryptographic, yeah, not one of my best. So moving on, perhaps the reason she asked about my work was that if I turned out to be a billionaire tech bro, she'd see it within herself to ignore my sartorial faux pas.

"Espionage," I said, existential nausea kicking in and already sensing that this event would not result in my making any contacts that would yield legal business. "You? I mean besides hosting the occasional fundraiser."

"I have the hardest job in the world," she said, proudly sticking out her perhaps surgically augmented chest.

"Sherpa? Navy SEAL? Bomb-sniffing dog? Trump press secretary?"

"Stay-at-home mom. Between my daughter, husband, and nanny, I'm bringing up three children."

I liberated a martini from the tray of a waiter—even they were wearing tuxedoes.

"Someone ordered that!" the hostess said.

"Please thank him, her, they—whatever pronoun's appropriate." After several gulps, I deposited the empty glass on another waiter's tray. "Suzie said this event is to increase awareness of climate change and, of course, to raise money to combat it. But somehow this crowd isn't giving off eco-friendly vibes. I haven't seen a fruit or vegetable since I got here, and the plethora of American flag lapel pins makes me fear that war's been declared while I was walking across the park to get here."

"Global warming is a libtard hoax." She curled her lip in disgust. "We're here to help make America great again."

"Good idea," I said. "But raising money to kill Trump seems legally questionable."

She looked at me like I had baby tarantulas crawling from my eye sockets.

"The libtards intend to tax us to death and put us in reeducation camps."

"Seems like overkill. I mean if we're already dead from . . . never mind." I scanned the room. "There's Suzie. Please excuse me."

I'd dated Suzie some years before, and we'd mutually decided that we'd rather be friends than lovers. Actually, on reflection, I now recall that had been solely her decision.

On my way to her, I snatched a baby lamb chop from another waiter, dipped it in mint sauce, and wolfed it down, getting only several drops of sauce on my T-shirt. If I'd worn a tux, I'd have needed a bib, or maybe an extra-large cummerbund would've been sufficient. Not making a pig of myself with all this food around wasn't an option. Seeing no place to put the bone, I substituted it for the celery stalk in a dowager's Bloody Mary. Either she didn't notice, or that was what one did at such events.

"Robert, what are you doing here?" Suzie said, turning from a man on the fatal side of fifty whose stomach hung over his cummerbund, to whom she had been talking or, more accurately, to whom she'd been listening to as he prattled on about how trickle-down economics fosters dynamic growth.

The man continued speaking, oblivious to the fact that Suzie was no longer looking up at him admiringly or even facing him.

"You invited me." I pointed the celery stick at her for emphasis.

"No, I invited you to the benefit for the Sierra Club. It's tomorrow night—same place, different night."

"Oh, my hyperaggressive spam filter devoured your invite before I could . . ." I again scanned the room, confirming my original impression that this group, reveling in their white privilege, was one in which I neither belonged nor wanted to. "But I don't get it . . . Are you a Trumpling now?"

"I'm politically agnostic. Just here looking to meet gullible rich men." She shrugged. "If they believe his bullshit, think of what I could persuade them to do."

"Makes sense. I'll leave you to it."

On the way out, I chugged a glass of forty-year-old single malt scotch I'd liberated from the tray of a passing waiter and wolfed down another baby lamb chop. Damn, another grease and mint sauce stain. If this keeps up, I'm going to have to wash my T-shirt after another two or three cocktail parties.

I won't even try to come up with an enticing lead-in to the next chapter. But not to worry—it's short, entertaining, and interesting. Hey, as a lead-in, that's not bad.

XXVI

European vs. US Medical Care: A Case Study

December 2018

In the year 2 BC (before COVID), while on vacation in Florence, Italy, with Amy and Adam, I tripped on a loose carpet on the way back from the bathroom and cracked my head open on the corner of a desk. It being 2:00 a.m. and not wanting to wake Amy, I wrapped a towel around my forehead and returned to bed. At daybreak, unsettled by my dilated, different-sized pupils and the blood-soaked towel, sheets, and pillows, Amy insisted that I seek medical attention. I declined; it would heal on its own. I didn't want to miss the Pitti Palace, didn't speak Italian, and wasn't comfortable with becoming ensnared in a foreign medical care system.

The hotel concierge told us that the Italian health service, the Servizio Sanitario Nazionale, would treat me free of charge. But as it was early on the Sunday before Christmas, I'd receive more attentive treatment at a nearby private clinic—from which he would undoubtedly receive a kickback. I opted for the health service. After giving my choice the consideration it deserved, Amy accompanied me to the private clinic.

On seeing the Palladian mansion surrounded by a lush garden, my eyes rolled back, replaced by dollar or, rather, euro signs.

Not having mastered the American technique of keeping patients waiting until they lose their patience, a doctor appeared in a few minutes. After examining me, he recommended a CT scan and plastic surgery. A troupe of euros danced Busby Berkeley–like before my eyes. Also, I didn't want to lose a day of our vacation. So I told him that since the bleeding had stopped, a Band-Aid and a Tylenol would be sufficient. He responded like a judge after hearing a drunk Rudolph Giuliani present a case of voter fraud, and Amy denied my appeal.

While the doctor roused a plastic surgeon from his Sunday morning repose, a technician administered the CT scan, which confirmed I was as hardheaded as I was hard-hearted. Shortly thereafter, the surgeon arrived, perhaps lured by the scent of money. He explained in clear English that I'd need an astronomical number of tiny stitches if I wanted to avoid a disfiguring Tony Montana–like facial scar. With the euro meter spinning at warp speed, I felt like a foreigner getting into a cab on Fifty-Ninth Street and being taken to Grand Central by way of the Grand Canyon. In my head appeared the image of me being lifted by my ankles and shaken until all my money fell from my pockets, having to leave the place clad only in a barrel. In any event, he proceeded with such competence that my scar is barely visible.

Blessedly, what would have taken a couple of days in the good ole US of A had been expertly performed in three hours from beginning to end, which only reduced the time until I'd have to confront the bill. What was the limit on my American Express card? Did Italy have debtors' prisons?

Amy reminded me she'd procured for us limited coverage via travel insurance, knowing that our medical insurance wouldn't cover foreign treatments. She'd already contacted them and been told that they would cover only what they deemed *reasonable and necessary*, insurance-speak for they'd pay bubkes.

As I approached the business office, I could practically hear my heart pounding. Perhaps they'd have the courtesy to offer me a blindfold and a cigarette.

They presented me with the bill.

I looked.

I gasped in disbelief. My concussion must have been worse than I thought. I blinked several times and looked again, but the number didn't change. Then it hit me like a grand piano falling from a billionaire's penthouse: it must be an Italian custom to leave out the final two zeros.

"Is this correct?" My voice trilled up like a high school nerd asking out the girl of his dreams.

"Sì, signore."

"But €356? That's, like, $425."

"Sì, I think so."

A few weeks later, I received, from Fly-By-Night Insurance Company Inc., a check for $998. Accustomed to US medicine, their computer program couldn't pay less than that for an examination, a CT scan, and plastic surgery without decomposing into a puff of smoke and a mass of undifferentiated 0s and 1s.

The moral: we don't know how bad we have it.

A couple of years later, as if to underscore that point, COVID hit; and the country wasn't prepared for it, but then again, neither was Italy. At least the Italians could die from the disease without first driving themselves into bankruptcy and impoverishing their progeny.

Oh, and speaking about disease . . .

XXVII

Horrendous Timing

March 2020

As I've said, within days of my retirement, the plague hit with pent-up fury. I dreaded tedium and lassitude that would accompany a lockdown more than the virus. Amy, however, had more conventional priorities. Declaring, "If I die, Adam will never forgive you," she reluctantly permitted one venture outside a day.

Much of what we did to protect ourselves from the disease in that early period seems excessive in retrospect or, rather, downright bonkers. Following the CDC's increasingly shambolic advice, we let our mail sit for three days before opening it so any viruses from postal workers or senders would lose their potency. Not that anyone ever died from junk mail, but perhaps poison-pen letters... When we finally opened it, we, following instructions, did so wearing latex gloves. Not feeling safe to go into stores, we had all our groceries delivered and, again wearing latex gloves, wiped each object down with a Lysol wipe before putting it away. The authorities told us to trust the science and take these precautions even though there was not a scintilla of scientific basis for any of them. The experts knew it was a respiratory virus, so it didn't spread via mail or cans of peas, so WTF. They also insisted that we wash our hands frequently for as long as it takes to sing

"Happy Birthday," a song that peer-reviewed studies must've unequivocally proven that viruses hate. Otherwise, they'd never have made such a silly-sounding suggestion. Finally, not stooping to admit that they were wrong, they slowly withdrew the most absurd of their guidelines. Perhaps, not knowing much about the virus, they were being ultra-conservative, but the result of their advice was that a significant portion of the populace became COVID paranoid, withdrawing from all social interaction; and schools were closed based on no statistical evidence that kids spread the virus to teachers. At the same time, many others lost all faith in governmental health officials and refused to get vaccinated as a matter of some principle too recondite for normal people to understand. They demanded full control over their bodies while denying women such control when it came to abortion.

In isolation, except for my daily solitary walks (where I wore a mask for no reason beyond a desire to show community solidarity and avoided coming close to any other pedestrians), I tried to maintain telephonic communications with the friends and acquaintances with whom I'd lunched, dined, or drank in the halcyon pre-COVID days. We, however, no longer had much to say to each other. My social life dwindled to conversations with telephone buddies. Once Amy slightly loosened my restrictions, I dragooned friends who resided in my neighborhood to take walks with me, with the understanding that we'd maintain a six-foot distance between us—surely just a coincidence that that was the depth of a freshly dug grave. Those telephone, and even the in-person, conversations grew tiresome, however. I became sick of mewling, or being mewled to, about Trump and COVID-19; and a conversational Gresham's law required that those two horsemen of the current apocalypse drove out more varied or stimulating topics.

I took classes on Zoom, but being remote, they neither fostered personal connections nor led to the new friendships. Zooming only added to my angst, ennui, and alienation and confirmed that I operated on a high bleak ironic frequency most people never heard.

I hoped that after the plague (if I were still alive and mentally competent), I'd reconstruct my social life. Perhaps I'd meet people who laughed when I'd said something I thought to be clever or, even better, who made me laugh. It'd been too long since I'd really laughed. I wasn't confident I could make that happen. Even under the best of circumstances, it wasn't easy to make new friends at my age, and the headwinds from COVID and the plague of political polarization made it even more difficult. Also, I feared that laughter, or at least my sense of humor, had gone out of style like hoopskirts or spats. That fear was reasonable as my sense of humor was never quite as stylish as those items were in their heydays. There had been numerous recent articles on the epidemic of loneliness, particularly for men of a certain age, leading to a spike in deaths of despair. So I wasn't the only one suffering. Indeed, my problems were insignificant compared to many other people's, but I've always found it easier to bear other people's problems than my own.

True to his habit of bootless, mean-spirited gestures, undoubtedly directed solely at me personally, Mayor de Blasio closed the tennis courts. So I started hitting balls against a handball court wall, which was marginally more satisfying than hitting the wall with my head. Then for no conceivable reason beyond that he had the power to do so, he locked down the handball walls and took the rims and nets off the basketball courts.

Grasping my last lifeline, I called a friend from law school who was an aficionado of my hyperbolic rants.

"I've got maybe ten good years left. Given Trump's and de Blasio's incompetence, I'll be spending at least one of them in confinement, like a convicted felon. Except that they're allowed daily trips to the exercise yard and the pure joy of shanking those who irritate them."

"You've got it a whole lot better than many people," he said with an edge finely honed to cut through bullshit.

"You're saying I can't even enjoy feeling sorry for myself. My god, things are even worse than I feared."

"Blaise Pascal said, 'All of humanity's problems stem from man's inability to sit quietly in a room alone.' If you can't be happy watching Netflix and reading, there's something seriously wrong with you."

Eschewing the traditional "with all due respect, blow it out your ass" and tapping into my wide, albeit shallow, reservoir of useless arcane facts, I said, "A dyspeptic insomniac, Pascal died at thirty-nine."

"My daughter's a respiratory therapist. People are dying all around her. I'm terrified for her." He hung up.

Having one less friend to worry about freed up more time for me to agonize about myself.

On my solitary walks, I observed couples holding hands, men frolicking with kids and dogs, happy and exuberant groups of friends dining alfresco in the parks or in restaurants' festive sidewalk extensions, and folks appearing to have adapted far better than me to the situation. Veiled in my literal and figurative masks, I felt as insignificant as a broken fire hydrant that even dogs wouldn't bother pissing on.

Struggling to occupy myself, I wrote the following. Although fictional and exaggerated, it accurately portrays my underlying angst—one of my few authentic feelings and one I shared with the majority of Americans:

When the going gets tough, the tough go for a walk.

Late afternoon, it's already dark. Because of financial cutbacks, the traffic lights and streetlights no longer function. A full moon, periodically eclipsed by rushing clouds, casts an intermittent foreboding light. Icing up, my mask flops with each breath like a prehensile gill.

Cars speed on icy, unplowed Riverside Drive, hoping the faster they go, the less time they'll be exposed to danger. A skidding SUV slams into a parked car and is in turn rear-ended—my big break as the pileup allows me to cross the street safely.

The week-old Slurpee of slush and grime makes footing treacherous, but I like the solitude until . . .

Jumping out of the way of a scurrying mischief of rats, I lose my balance and trip over the corpse of a huge black dog. A cloud of flies swarms up, revealing that it's not black, but a hairless, bloated, bloody pink. Flies in this cold? Yet another sign of the coming apocalypse.

In a massive DIY igloo, a feeble fire illuminates a tightly packed scrum of shivering homeless souls casting lean and hungry looks. A pack of emaciated feral dogs stare back. Like much else this winter, the confrontation will end badly.

Clouds part, revealing an unmasked, camo-clad, MAGA-hatted goon. Mayor de Blasio claims the horde that invaded to dissuade voters, destroy ballot boxes, intimidate the courts, and commit multitudinous felonies will disperse once the election is decided at the conclusion of the second series of court-ordered recounts. Little good his claim does me now—particularly if any truth were to ever emerge from his mouth, it would be an odd coincidence, unlikely to be repeated.

The thug unslings his assault rifle.

Abiding by Governor Cuomo's advice that running provokes them, I keep walking.

The gunman points his weapon at me.

Fear blurs my vision.

A shot!

I drop to the ground.

Turns out the shot came from a rival thug.

Taking advantage of the ensuing firefight, I turn and head for home.

"How was your walk?" Amy asks on my return.

"Uneventful, same ole, same ole. I'm bored. Let's do something dangerous like go out for dinner."

"Maybe we can order in, if we wipe down all the food containers and reheat everything in the oven," she says.

Sensing that I enjoyed it and wanting me to stop looking at her for entertainment, Amy suggested that I write more. Fine in theory, but what the hell would I write? The cliché "write what you know" wasn't helpful since I didn't know much. Then it hit me! I'd write about my favorite subject, the only one about which I was a true expert: me. So I began writing this autobiography, and it passed the time, sometimes quite pleasantly.

In addition to writing, I had some legal work, which helped keep me sane, if only relatively so. My largest client from my days as a full-time lawyer hired me as a part-time general counsel, paying the same hourly rate he'd paid when I had my firm. Since I was working from home without any employees or other overhead, every cent went directly into my pocket. As a result, I was making more than I was worth. I enjoyed the work. I just wished there was more of it.

Enjoyed was an oversimplification. Working at my laptop from my dining area table, without the associates or support staff I'd relied on at my firm, I handled, among other smaller matters, two cases—each of which involved transactions worth three-quarters of a billion dollars that had generated hundreds of thousands of pages of documents. With teams of Biglaw lawyers on the other side, I felt like I was faking it. I was terrified that I was in over my head and feared that I didn't have the capacity to properly conduct a full trial. I reminded myself that I'd always felt like I was faking it; and often, when actually faking it, I'd achieved surprising success. Cases almost always are settled, even those like the ones I was handling, where there seemed to be no possibility of an amicable resolution. So I hoped these would as well. If not, I could claim I had COVID and had to isolate myself.

Every year of my life, I'd celebrated Passover with my family. Since Amy and I got married, we either had a Passover seder with her sister's or my sister's family. Sadly, that tradition ended with COVID. Amy and I ate at home, with Adam participating via Zoom.

Downhearted and feeling like I had to do something more to recognize the holiday but not feeling competent to write a new translation of the Haggadah, I settled for the following fantasy:

Standing on Hallowed Ground

Ominous swirling black clouds. The Central Park North Woods is deserted and redolent with menace. A bush bursts into flame. Sure, I'll call 911. But first, a selfie. I approach the flame so it'll look like my hair is on fire in the photo. No rush to call as, strangely, the fire isn't consuming the bush.

BUSH

Draw not nigh hither: put off thy shoes from off thy feet, for the place whereon thou standest is holy ground.[48]

CHAN

Drop the Jacobean dialect. It sounds pretentious coming from shrubbery.

BUSH

I AM THAT I AM!

CHAN

Yeah, we all are. It's a tautology.

---

[48] All the bush's statements are from the King James Bible, book of Exodus.

BUSH

Say this to the people of Israel: "I AM has sent me to you."

CHAN

Oh, you're . . . [I swallow hard] With their fourth election in two years, Israel's not likely to listen to me. But hey, you should run. With your record of smiting, flooding, town destroying, killing firstborns, etc., you could position yourself as more kick-ass than Netanyahu. Don't identify with the ultra-Orthodox religious party, though. They're even crazier than you, and you'd alienate the center, not to mention virtually the entire world.

BUSH

I have surely seen the affliction of my people and have heard their cry by reason of their taskmasters; for I know their sorrows.

CHAN

Perfect! Keep the campaign slogans general. Avoid specifics. You might even win the Palestinian vote.

BUSH

I am come down to deliver them out of the hand of the Egyptians, and to bring them up out of that land unto a good land flowing with milk and honey.

CHAN

No, that won't end well. Everyone who's messed with the Middle East has made things worse. You in particular—no offense meant.

Fire flares up. Sulfurous odor of burning hair. Ouch! My eyebrows are gone.

Oh, I get it. You're speaking metaphorically.

BUSH

Go, and gather the elders of Israel together, and say unto them, The LORD God of your fathers, the God of Abraham, of Isaac, and of Jacob, appeared unto me, saying, I have surely visited you.

CHAN

I guess I could post something on Facebook and Twitter.

BUSH

What is that in thine hand?

CHAN

An iPhone. Steve Jobs is undoubtedly planning product launches in heaven as we speak.

My phone transforms into a snake, slithers off, and swallows a squirrel whole.

BUSH

I will stretch out my hand and smite Egypt with all my wonders.

CHAN [voice quivering with terror]
Oh . . . I'm not your first choice. You already have a plague in process, and I gather it wasn't a Jewish space laser that caused the California fires as claimed by Marjorie Taylor Greene.

There's a break in the swirling black clouds, and I see they're actually monstrous swarms of locusts. The Central Park North Woods Lily Pond turns bloodred and is surrounded by innumerable croaking frogs. This time, no hero will appear to lead us across a metaphorically parting Red Sea. God's appearance, like that of a certain rodent on another holiday, presages at least another ten weeks— months, years?—of the plague.

I've got to paint my firstborn's doorframe with the blood of an innocent lamb. If I hurry, Citarella, which touts itself as New York's premier seafood and fresh fish market, will still have some fresh lamb shank. Hopefully, Adam's Columbia University landlord won't treat it as a breach of his lease.

In September, seven months into the first plague year, I joined the Institute for Retired Professionals (IRP), where members took courses given by other members. They touted it as a way to make new friends. Maybe preplague it was and would be again postplague when classes would revert to in-person rather than Zoom. I had my doubts, though, as I, like many old people, don't like old people. Yet most of the members were quite bright and mentally sharp, and the group was so selective I was flattered that they accepted me. That first semester, I took courses in sixteenth-century Dutch art and Shakespeare power and politics as well as a writing workshop— all interesting. In the writers' workshop, we were given weekly prompts and charged with writing short pieces, either two hundred or five hundred words, depending on the assignment. Writing those pieces turned out to be among the more enjoyable things I did during COVID. Over winter break, I taught a course in comic writing, with mixed results as my students struggled to produce one piece per week, and I couldn't teach them how to do that.

The next semester, I continued with the writers' workshop, took a course on the Byzantine Empire, and taught one of four books that comprised a course in narrative nonfiction.

You're undoubtedly dying to hear more about my legal career. Please don't die on my account—at least not until you've recommended my book to all your acquaintances and written five-star reviews in your own names and multitudinous aliases on both Amazon and Barnes & Noble. But not to worry, we return to my legal career in the next chapter.

XXVIII

There Was Some Shit I Would Not Eat

April 2020

When I retired, David Ferber refused to let me use the only email address I'd ever had (chan@ferberchan.com) and refused to let me continue to use the firm telephone number, the only number many people I knew had for me. His rationale was that since I was no longer covered under the firm's malpractice insurance, my use of that email and telephone number could create a theoretical uninsurable liability for the firm if I were to commit malpractice while appearing to be practicing law under the firm's name. Never mind that I had no intention of practicing under the firm name, and unlike David, I'd gone more than four decades without a malpractice claim asserted against me.

The loneliness and dislocation of retiring into COVID had taken a huge emotional toll on me. I called David in tears, reminding him that we'd been friends and partners for more than forty years. He responded that he hadn't considered me a friend since I'd made our relationship "transactional"—Davidspeak for he was my friend only when he could exploit me by taking out of the firm far more than the value of his contribution, while I took out far less than I deserved. My father's adage that "a law firm is a collection of perfectly nice people who, put together, make one big bastard" once again rang true. Terrible that the little company I started with David grew into an entity that met that definition. Still, I understood that having become accustomed to living off my efforts, it pained him to go cold turkey. Just the same, I was angry; and with little else to do being in COVID lockdown, I allowed my resentment to metastasize. Whatever else one can say about rage, it does help pass the time even more pleasurably than self-righteousness.

Several months after my retirement, I learned that after I left the firm, David Ferber had pocketed more than $4,000 that one of my clients had paid the firm on a receivable that had been generated prior to my leaving.

I reminded David that under our partnership agreement, I had a contractual right to the money. He admitted that he'd also taken receipts that had arguably been due to a corporate lawyer and a trusts and estates lawyer who'd been forced out of the firm,[49] and he claimed those actions were a precedent for what he'd done here. I responded that, unlike those attorneys, David and I were parties to our partnership agreement under which I was entitled to the funds. He hung up so hard that it hurt my ear. Thereafter, he stonewalled me, failing to take my calls or respond to my emails.

A reasonable response would have been for me to sue him for the money. The amount involved, however, was too small to

---

[49] In the final decades of our partnership, I'd concentrated my efforts on building the firm's client base, handling litigation, and running the litigation department. Since his business deteriorated during that period, David had time on his hands, so he focused more on firm administration. I should've been more inquisitive about what he had been doing in the name of my firm. But after our long relationship, I trusted him and thought of him as a friend. Anyway, I had more than enough to do without getting involved in firm administration, which he was better at than me.

justify litigation; and I had no desire to be turned into a metaphoric bratwurst by the state court sausage-making machine.

An even more reasonable response, that of a fully evolved person, would have been for me to forget about David's misappropriation of funds and move on. The money wouldn't have changed my life. I was making more from my one part-time client than David was making while working full-time for the firm or, rather, while putting in the puny hours he considered to be full-time. So why not let him have a few crumbs?

Had I forced myself to step back and view the situation objectively, I'd have seen that there was some merit to his point of view. I knew from my career as a litigator that there were two sides to most disputes, even though both parties believed themselves to be right. Our dispute, like most, called for compromise, particularly as that would have allowed us to preserve our long relationship. I would've been happy to compromise, but he'd made that impossible by refusing to talk to me. The most mature thing would've been for me to forget about it and move on.

However, I was hurt, and the suppressed anger and resentment that had built up over the decades of what I'd viewed as David's exploitation finally erupted. I'd supported him over the course of our four-decade partnership, never taking out of the firm all the money to which, by any objective standard, I was entitled. I'd had it with eating his shit with respect to the division of the firm's profits, as described above. It offended me that he'd so improvidently destroyed our relationship for a relatively paltry sum. *Why the fuck should I have to be the reasonable one?* As you've already seen, I do the mature thing only after all else has failed. Also, it pissed me off that he thought he could get away with taking advantage of me and showing me so little respect that he seemed to believe it would be a successful strategy to cut all channels of communication by which we might have resolved our dispute via compromise. I'd spent an entire career training myself to be a junkyard dog. Also, like E. E. Cummings's "I Sing of Olaf Glad and Big," there was some shit I wouldn't eat. So I sent the following email to each of the clients I'd brought into the firm whom David continued to represent:

> It's my sad duty to warn you that, if you are still doing business with David Ferber, you need to exercise extreme caution. He has recently misappropriated funds to which he has no legal right and has twice been sued for malpractice. Because I have left the firm, I don't know whether purloining funds and inattention to his work have become his regular practice or whether they are isolated incidents. In any event, although an honest and highly competent person for almost all of our long relationship, he appears to have deteriorated in both respects. While I'm not in a position to offer any sort of medical diagnosis, it's conceivable that his recent erratic behavior might be explainable as an initial sign of dementia. I, of course, wish him well, but you need to be careful in your dealings with him.

While it was true that he'd been sued for malpractice (I never lie about anything verifiable),[50] it was unclear whether he'd done anything wrong beyond failing to cover his ass with a protective paper trail, as a more careful lawyer would have done. Both cases

---

[50] One of my three rules of how to be a successful liar. The other two are (1) lie as infrequently as you can and (2) remember all your lies.

had been settled within the limits of our malpractice policy without a ruling on his culpability.

That got David to email me:

> Despite your outrageous commentary to the contrary, we have always acted honestly and ethically in dealing with you. Nevertheless, your barrage of emails is so thoroughly distressing that I am sending you a check today . . . and with this payment, I hope to never have to communicate with you again. Do not respond to this email, do not communicate with me again, do not refer any clients.

For my relationship with the firm I'd founded with David in 1981 to end like that was disheartening and was undoubtedly one of the factors that imparted a negative cast to my memories of my legal career. Pandemic-induced isolation and concomitant low-key depression exacerbated those feelings. David's stupidity was perhaps even more disturbing than his cupidity. While I was semiretired, I wasn't dead. I knew many of the same people David did and had some valuable business contacts. Moreover, I was part-time in-house counsel to a company that spent more on legal fees (most of which went not to me but to large firms around the country) in a month than David and the other lawyers in the firm collected in a year and, on my say-so, could send them more corporate business than they could handle. Also, I was frequently asked for recommendations of lawyers. Indeed, after retiring (or rather semi-retiring), I'd referred substantial legal business to Bob Kaplan, my former litigation partner.

A primary casualty of my falling-out with David was the loss of his ne'er-do-well, failed stand-up comic son as my connection for marijuana, which, in those days, I took largely as a sleep aid.[51]

Hopefully, I'll learn a lesson about obsessing over a problem until I overreact and will, in the future, be more conscious of my tendency to fall into the trap of self-righteousness. It takes constant effort to change long-established patterns, and some backsliding has to be expected. At the rate I was improving, I'd achieve that goal by my 150th birthday.

And here comes a comic piece reflecting on COVID, sort of. Don't worry, it's short and entertaining if you happen to like that sort of thing.

---

[51] I also take Ambien, but I've seen studies that claim Ambien might increase the risk of getting Alzheimer's. As marijuana has been illegal, there have been no large-scale peer-reviewed studies of its long-term effects. Accordingly, there's no evidence it causes any material harm, and it does help me sleep in a rather pleasant way.

XXIX

La Maison de Après La Peste

April 2020

An assignment from my IRP writers' workshop: "When the pandemic is over, you plan to go to a restaurant that doesn't exist for a perfectly delightful meal. Tell us about the experience." I set forth below my response to that prompt not only because I find it amusing but also because it's evidence of how far the COVID restrictions had pushed me around the bend:

"I'm excited we're actually going out for dinner," I said to Amy as we approached the restaurant. "But having to submit NDAs and essays about what we missed most during COVID with our reservation application raised more red flags than a Stalinist May Day parade."

"Do you smell something burning?" she asked.

Had she always ignored my bellyaching, or was that a plague-related development?

"Vestige of last night's bonfire of the outdoor sheds." Restaurants had been permitted to construct ramshackle sheds on the sidewalks and stretching into the streets in order to expand their outdoor seating capacity when indoor dining had been banned.

The restaurant occupied the entire block, cheap real estate being a classic benefit of the plague. Its huge, sculptured brass doors resembled those of the Florence Baptistery, except instead of Ghiberti's Gates of Paradise, they recreated Hieronymus Bosch's The Garden of Earthly Delights.

The doors swung open. The joyful noise almost knocked us over. The light in the reception area was so bright that I felt as if, after a month in a pitch-black underground cave, I'd stepped out into the blazing noonday sun. The cavernous main dining room recreated the Salisbury Cathedral's nave on a scale of 1:3. Colored light beaming through stained glass windows divided the space into separate areas, each with a communal table.

"It's certainly festive. I'll say that for it . . . or against it," I said. "Thankfully, they wasted no money on good taste."

"Unlike you, they're sensitive enough to understand that we all now crave stimulation." Amy hadn't actually said unlike you. She hadn't needed to.

A hunky young man approached Amy, followed by a sultry blonde in an extraordinarily little skin-hugging black dress.

"Hi, Amy. I'm Jason. I'll take you to your table." He nudged her to his right, while Cassie, his partner, nudged me left.

"We'd like to share the experience together," Amy said.

"Everybody says that." Jason chuckled. "As if they expect us to believe they aren't sick of each other. Amy, as you miss haute cuisine and philosophic conversation, you'll be at La Table de Paris. Desiring debauchery flavored with discussion of classical history, Robert's at Mensa Romana."

Directing me toward the sacristy, Cassie said, "You can change across from the vomitorium."

She turned her back as I changed into a purple-trimmed toga. I liked that she peeked at me over her shoulder and refrained from retching.

"Our food is shared communally. And the serving girls and boys are of age, if just barely; disease-free; and very anxious to please," she said. "I recommend the dormice stuffed with pork, flamingo tongue tacos, and ostrich with herbed, spiced honey. The fermented fish sauce, though, isn't to everyone's taste."

"Sounds authentic." My tone communicated that I didn't consider authenticity a virtue. "I hope the wine's not mixed with water, like in classical times."

I regretted the toll the pandemic had taken on my sense of humor.

"You and your tablemates can choose the blend of sativa and indica for the communal hookah." She gave my nose a flirtatious finger tap. "The Château Haut-Brion 2000 and Viagra cocktail is recommended for your demographic."

"Not sure Amy would approve," I said, quite sure she wouldn't.

"Jason and friends will keep her occupied."

Except for the intrusions from EMTs carting away those whose hearts gave out from the unaccustomed excitement, it was an enchanted evening.

And now we return to the present, even if by the time you read this, it's four years in the past. As any student of Einsteinian astrophysics knows, time is a curious, bendy thing—if it can even be classified as a thing.

XXX

Saved by a Sewage Plant

May 2020

It's May 2020—three long, tedious, lonely months into the plague. I find the only four tennis courts open in all of New York City. They're in Riverbank State Park, a twenty-eight-acre recreational facility built on top of the gigantic sewage treatment plant that extends over the Hudson River between 136th and 142nd Streets. It's a lovely facility except for the occasional whiff of sewage. In addition to its four tennis courts, the park has basketball courts, a baseball field, a running track, an Olympic-sized swimming pool, a gym, an ice-skating rink, and backboards for practicing tennis strokes. Due to its West Harlem location, most New Yorkers have never heard of it, and few have ventured up to the park. As a state park, Riverbank isn't subject to de Blasio's bumbling jurisdiction and punitive COVID performance politics.

Outdoor tennis is COVID risk-free and provides healthy physical and psychic relief, but the reason the Riverbank courts are open has more to do with Cuomo's desire to undermine de Blasio than a desire to improve the people's quality of life. Still, actions count more than motives, particularly as actions are clear and motives hard to know.

The US Lawn Tennis Association (USLTA) has promulgated a series of foolish rules. They prohibit doubles (fine with me as I prefer singles), requiring each player to bring his or her own balls and write their initials on them and prohibiting players from touching any (tennis) balls other than their own. It also forbids changing sides at the conclusion of odd-numbered games (which has been done since the inception of the modern game to balance the effects of sun and wind). Other than the rule about doubles, the other restrictions are quickly disregarded as being silly and having no effect on the spread of the disease.

Hanging out at the Riverbank courts a few times and hitting against a backboard, I meet a group of singles players at my level with whom I enjoy playing.

Between the moderately hilly seven-mile bike ride up to the park and back and the hour of rigorous singles, I'm starting to get back into reasonable shape, and my mental well-being has entered a sustained bull market.

As I've said, Amy claims I suffer from ADHD. True or not, I have difficulty maintaining focus and concentration. The problem manifests itself in a variety of ways, including the way I learn. I manage to cover for it more or less. Since tennis is life, it serves as an apt example.

I've taken numerous tennis lessons over the decades, occasionally with renowned teaching pros. Often, they talk so much that my mind does a walkabout, or they give me so many tips that I can't focus on any of them. The most useful lesson I ever had was from a college kid whose prime job was maintaining the courts and helping run children's clinics. He told me just one thing: hit the ball more in front of your body. That made a huge difference. Even now, decades later when my game goes to shit, I remind myself of that advice. It often helps. Pros generally tell me to keep moving my feet and not to stand flat-footed, but that didn't sink in until I watched Federer play Nadal on TV. They also tell me not to change grips at net, but I've accepted that my habit is too ingrained for me to change it. So, knowing my limitations and realizing tennis is not my profession, I don't bother.

Tennis is simple, which is what makes it devilishly difficult. When Adam, at around seven years old, was learning the game, he said, "It's funny, in tennis, you're always learning the same things: watch the ball, bring you racket back early, move your feet." I once saw Serena play. When she was miked up, I heard her say to herself, "Watch the ball." After tens of thousands of hours of practice and world-class coaching, she was still working on the same simple little things that my son was when he first took up the game.

Over the years, I've developed several rules that help when my mind wanders and my game goes to shit:[52]

- Maintaining focus is more important than the mechanics of my strokes. I need to make myself concentrate on one thing—and only one thing—at a time, such as hitting the ball more in front, moving my feet, getting the racket back sooner, watching the ball, or hating my opponent, which often results in lifting my level of play to its normal mediocrity.

- Intensify the focus on the big points: ad-out, ad-in, set point.

---

[52] Note to my tennis partners: don't read the following bullet points.

- When playing well, take more risks, go for the lines. When not, concentrate on keeping the ball in play rather than trying to hit winners. Let the other guy make the mistakes. If he's not going to make mistakes, I won't beat him anyway.

- On the serve, it's one of two things: (1) keeping my head up at the time of contact and (2) tossing the ball high.

- Keep reminding myself that while winning is no big deal, losing is a horrific catastrophe.

- Never play with someone more than two decades younger than me.

Setting down the shit-colored glasses through which I habitually view the world, I allow myself to hope the plague will end before I enter my dotage as anything else is inconceivable. I have reason to hope that by the time the Riverbank courts close in November, Operation Warp Speed will have led to the creation and distribution of a vaccine. With that, combined with ramping up of testing and some version of herd immunity, the virus will go away on its own, as have past plagues; or maybe people will get so fed up with the restrictions that the government will be forced to lift them. Tennis courts weren't closed during the second-century Antonine Plague, the Black Plague, or the great cholera epidemic of 1831; and humanity survived—most of it anyway. Although during those plagues, particularly the Black Plague, Jews tended to get murdered en masse on charges that they poisoned the water, which these days would be seen by most people as a negative development.

Caution: angry rant to follow. I wrote the foregoing sentence before the October 6, 2023, Hamas terrorist attack spurred American students to chant "from the river to the sea" and "death to the Jews" and to terrorize Jewish students. While the brainwashed students condemn the most obscure mini microaggressions, they gleefully commit horrific macroaggressions while complimenting themselves on being *social justice warriors*. There are 195 countries in the world. Some like China, Myanmar, India, and many African nations treat the Muslims residing in their countries far worse than Israel treats the Palestinians. Assad murdered a million of his own citizens. Putin is trying to wipe out Ukraine, indiscriminately killing innocent civilians. The Sudanese are committing actual genocide (a word tossed out with abandon by leftist students to describe anything they don't like about Israel—ignoring the fact that Jews, unlike the Palestinians, were subject to an actual genocide). Yet these ignorant TikToked youngsters couldn't care less about such atrocities. Jewish lives don't matter to them. They demand boycotts of the one nation and only one, the only Jewish country. University presidents—who'd be horrified by calls to murder all Blacks, Latinos, or any other group—can't bring themselves to condemn the mass murder of Jews. Sure, if the woke brigade comes for me, I can make them dissolve into tears by addressing them with a pronoun they disfavor. But in 1923, everyone thought Hitler was a joke too. Makes me think of my paternal grandparents' relatives who remained in Germany and Austria because they considered themselves more German than Jewish. So much for safe spaces. Being Jewish means you can never feel totally comfortable in the land of your birth and your parents' birth[53].

---

[53] I have nothing good to say about Netanyahu and his incompetent, meanspirited right-wing government, or the mindless way they are pursuing their war against Hamas without having given practical consideration of an achievable end. That, though, doesn't justify antisemitism any more than opposing Putin's war should lead to violence directed at the Russian orthodox.

Sorry for the digression, but recent events have so enraged me that I can't control my anger. Actually, I'm not sorry. If you disagree, fuck yourself with a poison-coated seventeen-inch dildo.

Back to the present, which is now the past: When COVID begins to recede, I return to the subway, initially wearing a mask but soon not bothering to do so. Republican politicians, in league with the news media's efforts to capture viewers' attention, spread the canard that New York City in general and the subway in particular are cesspools of crime and that no one in their right mind who can afford an alternative mode of transportation should risk taking the subway. Never mind that crime rates in New York City, and particularly Manhattan and the subway, are far less than those in the red states.

In any event, the subway and its barely decipherable public announcements inspired the following:

I have to find someone to speak to . . . and quick. Frantic, I squeeze out of the train at the Times Square station. Not a cop in sight. Defying my aged knees, I jog down the platform and see no one who can help. Desperate, I reverse direction.

A train is about to pull into the station. People step away from the edge of the platform, clearing a path. I dart in front of a ranting homeless man, the type that gives schizophrenia a bad name.

I see a squat woman wearing a white shirt with an MTA (Metropolitan Transit Authority) shoulder patch and a red-and-orange reflective vest also bearing an MTA patch. Thank God!

I've almost reached her when she begins to mount the steps. Waving my arms and shouting, I get her attention.

"I need to talk to you." I fight for breath. "I was on the 3 Train." Sweat burns my eyes. "There was an important announcement: 'If you see something suspicious in the station or on the train, tell a police officer or an MTA employee.' I saw something suspicious, several somethings."

"We have a report of suspicious activity," she says into a walkie-talkie device.

"An obese man wearing a MAGA hat and a 'Jesus wasn't vaccinated' T-shirt asked a hipster for directions to the Empire State Building," I say. "The hipster told him to take the train to Thirty-Fourth Street."

She rolls her eyes. Does she really not understand how suspicious that was?

"He gave him the correct directions. Under normal circumstances, I would have expected him to send the Trumpling to 149th Street / Grand Concourse or another crime-ridden station," I explain even though I thought an explanation should've been unnecessary.

"Never mind," she says into her communication device.

"A woman wearing a white dress—even though it's well after Labor Day—had a pastrami sandwich with mayo on white bread," I say to the MTA bureaucrat. "She was reading Finnegans Wake and smiling as if actually enjoying it. Not merely suspicious, these are signs that we're staring into the abyss."

Inexplicably, even faced with this irrefutable evidence of something suspicious, the MTA lackey turns to leave.

I grab her vest.

"It wasn't merely a run-of-the-mill announcement, but 'an important announcement' from the NYPD."

She bats my hand away.

"Did you see the homeless guy I ran in front of as a train was approaching?"

That gets her attention—finally.

"He didn't push me onto the tracks. Surely, that's suspicious."

Likely not an actual MTA employee, but an impostor afraid of being exposed, she walks away.

Announcement on my return trip: "We're being held momentarily by the train's dispatcher." Half an hour later, train still stalled, I'm sardined against an unwelcome diversity of fellow travelers and subjected to the sickening stench of the unwashed mixed with that of the excessively perfumed.

Another announcement: "We're delayed because of a sick passenger in a train ahead of us. Please be patient."

New Yorkers expected to be patient? Talk about suspicious.

"Who the fuck does the malingerer think he is? Why can't he get sick on his own fucking time?" says a permatanned woman, her skin stretched tight by a surgeon's knife. "Roll the selfish prick onto the track and get going."

Merciful God. We've stepped back from the abyss.

Meanwhile, the plague restrictions ease up somewhat. Amy spends the summer on Fire Island, and I spend five nights a week there. Doubles still verboten, I play singles several times a week, which I prefer. I also swim distances and kayak in the Great South Bay. Our house, although quite modest, is one block from the ocean; a block and a half from the bay, the tennis courts, and the baseball field; and about a half mile from the one store in our town. Everything has to be close together on Fire Island as no cars are allowed, so people ride bikes and walk, sometimes pulling little red wagons if they need to haul something. Amy's sister and brother-in-law also have a house out there, and I enjoy their company and that of their children and grandchildren.

Also, to a limited, but pleasurable extent, I get to interact with nature on Fire Island—turtles, rabbits, squirrels, and deer abound. The deer had been a major problem because they snacked in people's gardens and carried Lyme disease ticks. But they ceased to be a problem once the town instituted a contraceptive program for the deer—oral contraceptives mixed with their food since it would've been difficult to fit them with condoms or to persuade them of the virtues of abstinence.

More about that later. It's time for me to settle scores with someone who conspired to make my plague time more miserable than it needed to be.

XXXI

COVID Good News

November 2020

Although back to playing tennis, I continue to nurse a grudge against de Blasio. What conceivable reason could he have had for shutting down the handball walls? One of the only pieces I wrote, after I was able to return to tennis and other activities, was the following COVID-driven fantasy to assuage my feelings about the mayor—THE FUCKING GUY CLOSED THE TENNIS COURTS . . . UNFORGIVABLE. I took it personally. As I'm a person, I don't know how else to take it.

A live news truck, with GNN (Good News Network) emblazoned on its side surrounded by a profusion of the network's smiley-face logos, is parked in Battery Park, at the southern tip of Manhattan. An attractive reporter stands nearby, holding a microphone. The smiley-face logo adorns her mask; and everything about her—from her sunny, yellow pumps to her sunny, yellow short skirt and skimpy jacket to her long sunny, blonde hair and sparkling gold-flecked eyes—radiates a cloying enthusiasm that some find infectious, others merely nauseating.

"Felicity Apple of the Good News Network here on this perfect peach of a day to cover the Blue Angels flyover honoring the heroic nurses and doctors who are working night and day to keep us safe."

A black cloud darkens the sky, and a gust of wind blows a page from yesterday's New York Post onto her face, which she removes with a joyous flick of her hand and continues speaking without missing a beat.

"It's wonderful to see this well-mannered crowd, all wearing masks, observing social distancing, and thoroughly enjoying themselves."

She holds out her microphone to a passing woman.

"Ma'am, I couldn't help but notice there's a hole in your mask. May I give you a new one?"

"No," the woman says. "I cut away the mouth and nose to make it easier to breathe."

"But . . . ," Felicity says. "Stay safe. Keep extra distance. Enjoy the fantastic day."

The woman walks on. After several rapid shakes of her head, the twinkle returns to Felicity's eyes. But her gold-flecked contact lenses have moved, revealing a brown iris.

"One of the many, many feel-good stories that almost makes this horrid plague bearable is the glorious return of wild animals to the deserted city streets."

The camera pans to huge black birds riding the updrafts and a pack of unidentified mammals. Felicity approaches a passing man.

"Sir, isn't the return of these wonderful animals just the best?"

"Those vultures carried off a child the other day, and I can do without hyenas feasting on any dogs they can run down. As for the swarms of rats with the restaurants closed . . ."

"Well, what an absolutely scrumptious day for the flyover, right?"

The man shrugs and walks on. Looking into the camera, Felicity tosses her head back, an incongruously flirtatious gesture, then stands straight.

"Oh, look! There's Mayor de Blasio!"

As everyone other than his police escort is avoiding him like the plague, she has no trouble approaching.

"Mr. Mayor, what do you think of this great crowd, this wonderful event?"

As he's 6'5", all that's visible of Felicity are her mic and strands of windblown blonde hair.

"Always time for the press, Felicity. If these people don't maintain social distancing, we're going to keep the city locked down until the current generations die off and are replaced by ones that obey rules. We've already closed all the schools and playgrounds. Bars may be next."

He makes eye contact with a policeman and tilts his head toward a maskless couple holding hands. The cop separates them with a swing of his billystick. The mayor turns away to avoid seeing the woman getting knocked down, blood pooling around her head.

"Keeping us safe, a constant struggle for our ever-vigilant leader," Felicity says, her tone sounding forced.

"I have an exciting announcement," the mayor says, more enthusiastic than even Felicity had been when beginning her report. "I'm renewing my campaign for president because I'm the only one capable of progressively handling this pandemic while defunding the police."

Felicity stifles a laugh when she realizes he wasn't joking.

"Well, that is exciting," she manages to say, voice sapped of energy.

The mayor and his entourage ascend a makeshift viewing stand. With crenellated walls and gun loops, it resembles a high castle. De Blasio waves. Several respond with a middle-finger salute.

The Blue Angels come into sight. Some in the crowd look up; some don't bother.

"Wow! And I mean WOW!" Felicity shouts reenergized as if she'd been plugged into an electric socket. "Here come the jets! It's miraculous how they maintain such close formation . . ."

Fear appears in her eyes. "It almost looks like their wings touched, and a piece of wing came off. It'd be fascinating to learn how they create that illusion."

One of the planes begins spinning uncontrollably. It heads toward the viewing stand, smoke pouring from its engines.

"Oh my god! Oh my god!"

A huge explosion. The scene is obscured by black smoke.

The crowd stampedes. The smaller, frailer ones get trampled. One of the runners looks behind him. The viewing stand and everyone on it have been obliterated. He stops, raises a celebratory fist, and shouts with joy.

Others do the same. No longer fleeing, the crowd erupts in frenzied cheers.

"Here's the good news, and you're hearing it first on GNN—New York's about to get a new mayor!"

As I have a personal grudge against de Blasio, it can be claimed that I'm not an impartial observer. Objectively, he's an extraordinary politician. By an astounding act of political legerdemain, he managed to earn the loathing of the right, left, center, and politically indifferent. Even the municipal unions and big political contributors to whom he kowtowed to the detriment of the city can't abide the man. As for the colossal harm closing the schools (for no discernible reason beyond sucking up to the teachers' union) did to the children of the city, particularly the disadvantaged, don't get me started. Well, I've already started. But having vented my spleen, I'm ready to return to Fire Island and a curious incident.

XXXII

Twenty-First Century Fox

July 2021

As I always do when I arrive, I leave my blue sneakers by the side door to our beach house. We have white floors, and for some inexplicable reason, Amy wants them to stay that way. The next morning, the sneakers aren't there.

At least I think I'd left them by the door. Is this a sign of dementia, like putting the ice cream in an underwear drawer or wandering around the neighborhood naked? No, the sneakers aren't in the freezer, microwave, or medicine cabinet; and I'm fully, if unfashionably, dressed. Did a fanatical fan purloin them as a trophy? No, I don't have fans, let alone fanatical ones. But if I had groupies, I hope they'd be sex-crazed plaster casters,[54] not shoenappers. Is the Almighty playing a cosmic prank? No, he'd condemn my immortal soul to everlasting hellfire, give me leprosy, screw with my backhand, or have me tear a tendon just when I finally got my postretirement, postplague life together.

Two days later, my sneakers appear in the Lyme-disease, deer-tick breeding farm that serves as our backyard. What the . . . ?

---

[54] Groupies who, after bedding rock stars, made plaster casts of the musicians' private parts, which, in the case of those rock stars, weren't all that private.

Then while eating breakfast, I see a red fox snatch my son's blue shorts from the drying rack. Mystery solved. Adam's shorts, though, never reappear.

My annoyance morphs into acceptance. For there to be cross species understanding, we must be supportive of vulpine sartorial aspirations and the like. After all, a fox, in his blue period, can't order an azure deerstalker hat from Amazon or purchase cerulean socks at Paul Stuart.

And so let's return to New York City, the navel of the universe.

XXXIII

The Late Robert Chan

September 2021

With the return of clement weather, I return to biking, in Central Park, Riverside Park, and up Riverside Drive to the Riverbank tennis courts.

Lao Tzu notwithstanding, not every journey begins with a single step. Mine begins in my building's basement storage room. Sensing that I'm running late, my high-tech bike lock jams. Whose idea was it to make everything smart? Maybe I'm a few atoms short of a critical mass, but I can still outsmart most inanimate objects. I make a dejected face, hang my head, and turn to leave. Having lulled it into a false sense of victory, I spin around and unlock the damn thing before it has a chance to think.

The building's heavy security door and electric lock require two hands, but I need one to hold my bike and the other to open the door. With the dexterity of a person a decade younger than myself, I slip through before the door slams closed with the finality of a falling guillotine blade.

I have fifteen minutes to make the twenty-two-minute mostly uphill ride from Seventy-Eighth and Riverside to the 138th Street Riverbank State Park tennis courts. Would the world end if I were to arrive seven minutes late? I'm not going to risk the destruction of life as we know it, so I pedal on.

Also sensing that I'm late and conspiring with my smart lock, the Seventy-Ninth Street traffic light turns red just as I reach the corner. One has to respect the effort that went into programming the lights to maximize my inconvenience. I feel guilty that others are inconvenienced as collateral damage from the evil scheme to delay me.

Not bothering to downshift, I double-time it up the hill to Eighty-Ninth Street. A heart attack would throw off my schedule, but fortes fortuna juvat—fortune favors the bold.

I make up time by running the lights between there and Ninety-Sixth Street; after all, they're only advisory. But if someone were to get in my way by crossing against the light, fuck 'em.

I'm zooming downhill.

A cab door opens in front of me!

I swerve.

A horn honks; tires squeal.

Good, I need that shot of adrenaline.

The Ninety-Sixth Street light turns red, but I think I'm going fast enough to make it through before cars enter the intersection, honking horns and squealing tires cheering me on. A calculated risk: I need the momentum for the long uphill to 106th Street.

An oncoming black car crosses the yellow line to pass a bus. Ten inches in the wrong direction and my bicycle, frame and wheel bent, would've ended up painted a ghostly white and chained to a street sign—a somber memorial to the late Robert Chan.

A high school girl on an electric bike comes up alongside me.

"Do you have any old tennis balls? I need them for an art project," she says, apparently noticing the racket handle sticking out of my backpack.

"Sorry, no."

Her concerned facial expression communicates that my death rattle is all she hears. Turns out she isn't on an electric bike. *How the hell did she catch up to me?* She must be an Olympic-level athlete . . . or more likely just a reasonably fit person one-quarter my age.

Finally, I make it to the long downhill.

"Hey, that's a red light!" A goody-two-shoes vigilante grabs at my handlebars.

Lacking empathy, he's probably never been late for a tennis game.

Tragically, no devastatingly clever retort comes to me.

Dripping with sweat, my thighs cramping, I make it to the courts on time.

My opponent shows up a full three minutes late. Incredibly, he doesn't apologize.

A funny thing: Amy claims I'm a type A personality unduly hung up on time and the fear of being late. Well, even she can't always be right.

It gets too cold for bike riding, but the plague soldiers on.

XXXIV

Green Shafts of Hope and Perceptions of Risk

November 2021–September 2022

I previously wrote, "I allow myself to hope the plague will end before I enter my dotage as anything else is inconceivable." But now the inconceivable has become all too conceivable. Even though I live by the adage that one can never go wrong giving everyone the detriment of the doubt, I still vastly overrated the competence of the powers that be when it came to controlling the plague and, among other things, naively believed they wouldn't put the children's well-being over the paranoid, evidence-free whims of the teachers' union. I also underrated the virus's plucky tenacity.

Riverbank State Park and the late-opening city courts close for the winter, and the second—or third or maybe it's the fourth—wave of the virus hits with a vengeance, worse than ever in most of the country. New York City has yet to experience a repeat of the deluge of cases that overwhelmed its hospitals in April of 2020, but the more knowledgeable authorities say just give it time. If the competence of the three horsemen of ineptitude—Trump, de Blasio, and Cuomo—is all that protects us from devastation, we're headed for disaster.[55]

A more serious issue, however, is that Amy nixes my traveling to my indoor tennis club due to the risk—minimal in my view—of taking the subway, buses, taxis, Ubers, or rickshaws. After hard negotiation, she reluctantly gives me permission to play tennis indoors one day a week, but I have to walk or bicycle the three-plus miles to the Sixty-First and Second Avenue tram to Roosevelt Island. Although I recognize that she's compromised with me and that no one really knows what to do to avoid the disease, I still view her diktat as unreasonable. Yet I comply with only occasional lapses. Does that mean I'm a dutiful, respectful husband or a pussy-whipped wimp? That question is a perfect example of the multitudinous issues that should never be examined. A useful corollary to the first rule of cross-examination—never ask a question you don't know the answer to—*is never ask yourself a question to which you don't want to know the answer.* My god, did you ever think you could learn this much from a single book?

One cold and sleety day, I take the Seventy-Ninth Street Crosstown bus. As I'm fully vaccinated and masked and nonvaccinated passengers are not permitted aboard, the bus is COVID-safe. Walking the New York streets is more dangerous, particularly as pedestrian fatalities have spiked with the pandemic. Biking is yet more dangerous, a situation exacerbated by the invasion of unlicensed silent electric motorbikes and motorized

---

[55] As it turns out, the United States suffered more than most any other developed country. Perhaps that's the fault of the coterminous plague of unfathomable stupidity that afflicted those who refused to take the vaccine out of fear that the vaccine would cause their testicles to become as large as cantaloupes or that the vaccination drive was a conspiracy concocted by Bill Gates to implant microchips in people, as if they couldn't already be traced by their phones and even their refrigerators.

scooters oblivious to traffic lights,[56] speed limits, and one-way signs. Therefore, my decision to take the bus rather than walk conforms to the spirit of Amy's diktats rather than their literal words since she wants me to be safe. Have I mentioned humanity's unquenchable capacity for rationalization? Just because I recognize the problem doesn't mean I can't indulge in self-justification from time to time. That would be unfair, and I'm all about fairness, at least when it comes to myself.

As I walk down Second Avenue, having disembarked from the bus, Amy calls on my cell phone, asking what it was like walking through Central Park in the icy conditions.

I tell her, "Not too bad," which is true as it looked okay from the bus as we passed through on the Seventy-Ninth Street Transverse.

Then she closes the trap. A friend of hers had seen me get off the crosstown bus and ratted me out. *What were the odds of that? Did she have spies posted all over the city?*

That experience is an unpleasant echo of the time, over the summer, when Amy was on Fire Island. My fraternity brother and drag racing pal, Mark, came to town; and we went out for dinner in SoHo. He had the waiter take our picture, which he posted on Facebook. Although not on any social media, Amy somehow saw the photo and realized we'd eaten inside. I should've anticipated that. If the Chinese Communist Party had her surveillance capabilities, we'd all be speaking Mandarin and composing worshipful panegyrics and praise poems to President Xi.

I hadn't actually told her that we would eat outside, but I didn't tell her otherwise. I feel terrible about lying to her earlier and misleading her now, but her restrictions do tend toward the

---

[56] Traffic lights aren't *only advisory* when it comes to people other than myself.

unreasonable. I analogize it to Prohibition, which increased drinking. No, that won't fly. I was in the wrong. How about "to err is human; to forgive, divine"? Yeah, let's go with that one.

Marriage isn't easy, particularly when one of the parties is an asshole—and I don't mean Amy, who is anything but and has to put up with more shit than she deserves.

Running late to meet a friend and needing to wear a mask, I realize I'd forgotten my mask. I don't have time to return to my apartment. I see a mask on the street someone had discarded. After checking that it's dry and not stained with snot or blood, I put it on— the worst thing I can do from the perspective of COVID or even that of general hygiene. I hope Amy never learns of this. Maybe she won't read this far in this autobiography. I'm glad I had the foresight to set forth earlier the long description of my sexual escapades; that should bring her reading to a screeching halt.

I'm not blaming Amy for being overly restrictive. It's in her nature to be cautious, perhaps overly so, while I'm a tad reckless— perhaps several tads, one of the many advantages of the unexamined life. Hard to know the exact dimensions of a tad. But in any event, she, for example, wouldn't have hitchhiked across the country, gone to Aspen to study for law school finals, or started her own law firm without having first signed up several clients. Reasonable people differ vastly in their perceptions of risk. The odds of dying from a shark attack are lower than the odds of dying from having a TV fall on you. Yet many people stay out of the ocean for fear of sharks, but no one refuses to watch *Jaws* on TV because of the falling-TV risk. During the height of the AIDS epidemic, the risk of getting the disease from an act of unprotected sex between two people in low-risk groups was less than that of dying from a traffic accident due to driving six miles. Plenty of people were refusing to have sex out of fear, but as far as I know, no one turned down sex because it would've required driving more than six miles. Wait, thinking back on it, I recall that several women who lived more than six miles away from me spurned my ardent advances. Maybe that had nothing to do with my erotic appeal but was entirely based on the mileage that separated us.

I don't have a reasonable explanation for why I'm not concerned about COVID. Of course, I have my rationalizations; you wouldn't expect any less from me. For example, although over seventy and thus in a high-risk group, I'm in good shape and rarely ill. So I must have had a vigorous immune system. Therefore, I tell myself that if I get it, I'll have a mild case. Intellectually, I recognize that COVID is a quirky disease, killing and sparing indiscriminately. But risk perception is more emotional than intellectual. Intellectual analyses, such as those performed by the benighted souls who lead examined lives, serve only as cover stories utilized to cloak the brain's emotional responses in a patina of logic. On the other end of the COVID risk perception continuum, Amy is convinced that if she gets it, she'll die. Yet she continues to smoke cigarettes despite that well-documented risk. Hardly a groundbreaking observation that, with the exception of me and a handful of others, people are strange.

So that seamlessly leads into the subject of confronting fear.

XXXV

Nothing to Fear, Least of All Fear Itself

September 2022

I finally emerge from COVID isolation, ravenous for new experiences and human interaction. Recognizing that COVID has been traumatic for me,[57] Amy suggests I try improv. I demur. But she persists, as she's wont to do, telling me that being intimidated would be a step-up from my terminal boredom. Better to feel something than nothing, even if that something is unnerving or even unpleasant.

An internet search turns up the Magnet Theater, one of the few venues that have survived the plague. According to its website, it is

> a performance space and training ground for the best and brightest comedic talent in New York City. Since 2005, we've been at the epicenter of the city's growing improv movement—and today, we're one of the most recognizable improv schools and theaters in the city.

---

[57] I'm spending a perhaps inordinate time on COVID in this memoir, but it had a devastating effect on my psyche and set me up for the deep depression that was to come later. And although most people would like to forget it, the plague was a historically significant event that shouldn't be forgotten. When the next plague hits, we should be able to respond based on what we learned from this one.

As I have no acting experience, I'd prefer a training ground for the average, dimmest comedic "no-talents." However, not finding one of those, I sign up for a level 1 class at Magnet.

On my arrival at class, the enormity of my mistake hits me like a clip block from a sprinting NFL linebacker. Most of my classmates are one-quarter my age. They have acting experience, have come to New York in search of stardom, and seek to hone skills I never had and never will have.

To allay our concerns, the teacher, who's less than half my age, tells us that improv isn't primarily about wit, cleverness, or quickness. It's more about listening and reacting, which one already does every time one has a conversation. His words, however, have the opposite effect on me. I've been counting on my cleverness and quickness to see me through. Also, as I think Amy says, listening isn't one of my strong points. I can't be sure, however, as I don't always pay such close attention.

My misgivings notwithstanding, the class coalesces into a friendly, supportive group. Performing without a script turns out to be far more rewarding than terrifying, at least in this nurturing class setting. Rather than standing alone onstage, we work with partners, each of us intent on making the other one look good. When we click, it's thrilling. When we don't, it's okay and not embarrassing.

For our final class, we put on a public show—so much for a nurturing class setting. The butterflies in my stomach morph into vampire bats. *What if nothing comes to me; and I'm frozen in place, mind blank, stranding my scene partner?*

The show turns out to be a great success. The audience laughs enthusiastically and seems to appreciate my cleverness and quickness, notwithstanding that improv isn't primarily about that.

There are few more satisfying experiences than confronting terror and emerging triumphant. I'm high on accomplishment. When I come down, I crave another dopamine hit.

The playful, nonthreatening improv environment has helped to revive my sense of fun and spontaneity, both of which have been in short supply. In addition, improv helps me decrease overthinking and become more confident.

I've since taken three more improv courses and performed in three additional shows. One problem that arose is the improv company's effort to make sure we're performing in a *safe space*. To accomplish that end, they inexplicably ban routines centered on sex or politics—that is, 98 percent of my sources of humor and intellectual interest. They've even admonished me not to wear my "Make comedy offensive again" T-shirt. No one knows or can bear to contemplate what terrible, irreversible psychic trauma such jokes would have on the fragile twentysomethings' minds. Perhaps bathed in college's left-wing, wokish, anti-Semitic agitprop, their brains are now so delicate that anything that even subtly calls into question their brainwashing will cause them to shatter like a crystal brandy snifter hit by a piledriver.

Also, to my misfortune, my autobiographical writing and the calamitous concomitant need to analyze my past somewhat undercut the benefits of practicing improv. Had I been less quick to act and paused to consider the consequences of self-examination, I'd never have started this damn autobiography. Of course, if I'd been more introspective, thoughtful, and cautious, my life would have been materially different. Perhaps I'd have been so successful that someone else would write my biography. *The Great Chan* or

Chan: His Life and Times or *Chan the Man* or even *Chan and the Achievement of Permanent World Peace* would be catchy titles. But alas, it was not to be.

I've decided to stop writing. Lockdowns are over. I'm playing tennis, getting together with friends, and taking courses. Who needs it? Certainly not me and probably not you.

I'm in a wheelchair. Amy pushes me to the locked entrance gate of a dilapidated nursing home. Vultures circle, bats swoop, black storm clouds swirl, lightning flashes. She leaves me outside the gate without a kiss or word of farewell.

I wake depressed, lonely, terrified—my pillow wet with tears. It wasn't *just a dream*; it feels like a prophecy. I stifle tears. I don't want to wake Amy; she wouldn't come comfort me.

Having COVID, I've been banished to Adam's former room, now a storeroom crammed with boxes and unhung art. It stinks of urine as I have to pee in a bottle rather than infect the bathroom with the virus. Amy leaves food at the door. It has an unappetizing metallic taste—from Paxlovid, a symptom of the disease, or an effect of depression? Unlikely that she's poisoning me. She's too smart to use a toxin I could smell or taste.

I have a sore throat and cough but otherwise feel fine physically. That I'm fully capable of activity makes the mandatory isolation more intolerable.

Three days of solitary confinement down, seven more to go. I restrain myself from carving hash marks into the walls to mark each passing hour. I have books and a computer on which to watch TV and talk on the phone, but such windows to life outside bring me no pleasure as they serve to only highlight what I'm missing. Perhaps despondency is a side effect of the illness or the drugs. But it feels like a harbinger of a terrifying future, when I'll be too debilitated for physical activity and too demented for satisfying intellectual stimulation—alone, abandoned, bored, sad. On top of everything else, I'm a wimp and a coward.

COVID-isolation-driven boredom has brought me back to my computer to write the foregoing chapter, but now I really am done.

XXXVI

Groin Problems and a Meditation on the Nature of Happiness

October 2022

As all but the most dull-witted of you have already noticed, this autobiography didn't end with the previous chapter. Instead, I rescued it from the recycle bin. A new round of enforced inactivity, this time due to medical issues, compels me to again take up writing as an antidote to boredom.

Once people reach a certain age, things start to disappear due to the insidious activity of evil gremlins. Glasses, keys, and phones evaporate when we turn our backs, only to coalesce in places where we'd already looked multiple times. Also, we often find ourselves looking for phones utilizing the phone's flashlight app or madly searching for glasses we're already wearing.

I not only misplace the usual items but also lose my habitually worn shit-colored glasses. The COVID plague faded, and I gave up writing to avoid all future introspection and free up time for less laborious pursuits. I packed my schedule with activities—singles tennis and Ping-Pong three or four times a week each, as well as improv and IRP (now inexplicably bearing the meaningless name LP^2) classes, which are transitioning from Zoom to in-person. Also, my part-time legal work continued apace. In short, I cobbled together a busy, happy, engaging, and satisfying life—the details of which I saw no reason to share with you.

There'd been a number of recent widely publicized studies concluding that a major component of a long, healthy, and happy life is frequent interaction, preferably face-to-face, with friends, relatives, and even strangers. That I relied on studies rather than simply doing what made me happy said a lot about me—none of it good. In any event, I made it a point to have a meal, drinks, or a walk with one friend or another at least three times a week. Still concerned about COVID and less social than me even in the most salubrious situations, Amy didn't accompany me, but she blessed my going out without her. She had less need to socialize in person than me as she spoke with Adam and various friends on the phone several times a day, including one particular pal who was incapable of making a decision, responding to an email, or writing a text without consulting Amy.

Even Amy started to loosen up. We went to theater with another couple—we'd bought the tickets eight months earlier on the sure and certain hope that the plague would be done by now. The four of us had dinner before the show. At Amy's insistence, we ate outside under heat lamps. Our heads were too warm while our feet froze, but on average, we were comfortable. The theater required masks and proof of vaccination, but the ushers handled the crowd efficiently, and the audience was infectiously enthusiastic. It was wonderful to be out socializing. Maybe we'd do it again before I die or succumb to dementia.

Without my shit-colored glasses, I've slowly come to the astounding realization that I was happier than I'd been in almost any other time of my life. These times were made sweeter by the fact that the sword of Damocles of old age hung over my head by a fraying thread. Once my health or mental or physical capacity deteriorates, things won't be so rosy, so I'd better make the best of things while I can.

Then my life took an abrupt, albeit temporary, downward turn. I got a hernia and agreed to have an operation even though I knew that no one should ever go to the hospital unless totally healthy.

Before they wheeled me into the operating room, Amy and I met with the surgeon, only three hours after the time for which the surgery had been scheduled. If lawyers treated their clients as inconsiderately as doctors treat their patients, they'd have no clients. How doctors get away with overscheduling and triple or quadruple booking their patients (thus guaranteeing multihour waits) is, like most things these days, beyond me.

The doctor asked if we had any questions.

I shook my head, and to no surprise, Amy said, "I do."

"I know," the surgeon said, anticipating her question. "How long until he can resume sexual relations?" Whether she was joking or responding to her most commonly heard inquiry, I couldn't tell, either because she wore a mask or because my ability to understand the latent content of in-person communications had atrophied due to disuse.

Amy's one question turned out to be several—all practical and well-thought-out, not that I expected any less from her. She's far more thorough and detail-oriented than me in spite of my legal training and maybe due to my supposed ADHD. She wanted to know about wound care, pain management, and resumption of normal activity. Unsurprisingly, sex hadn't crossed her mind.

Sex, of course, crossed my mind—not that it had ever left there. Although I liked the way the surgeon's scrubs clung to her butt, I failed to turn that into an appropriate question. Indeed, even with the benefit of esprit de l'escalier (literally *staircase wit*), I couldn't come up with an appropriate comment along those lines. I'd lost my edge.

The operation went fine, but I'm not allowed to play tennis or Ping-Pong for six weeks. Not only do I enjoy playing both, but of at least equal importance, they occupy time and provide much-needed social contact, even if the accompanying conversations tend toward the superficial. It might be *only* six weeks, but it feels like years. What percentage is that of the time I have left as an able and active person?

With nothing better to do, I return to this autobiography, hence the switch to present tense again as I'm writing pretty much in real-time. Pneumonia has been referred to as "the old man's friend" since it kills after a short painless illness, allowing its victims to escape the dreary gradations of decay so distressing to themselves and their friends and family. Although I'm hopefully far from death's door, writing has an analogous positive effect on my emotional state since it allows me to transcend dreary boredom. Weak analogy—I have lost my edge.

While otherwise healthy, I've had an inordinate number of surgeries—two total knee replacements, a hip replacement, an Achilles tendon repair, cataracts in both eyes, a repaired broken finger, and two hernia operations. After the double knee-replacement surgery, I'd gone from the hospital to two weeks of rehab and left walking with a cane. I recuperated, enduring extensive painful physical therapy, while Amy and Adam enjoyed Fire Island during the summer between his junior and senior years in high school. I was back on the tennis court in three months. The hip replacement resulted in another three months without tennis but didn't require PT. The Achilles tendon was the worst—nine months without tennis.

I tore it in November 2015. By that June, I was finally out of the surgical boot. We went to China to celebrate Adam's high school graduation, and at my surgeon's suggestion, I wore cowboy boots so my heel would be elevated. I wore them with shorts because it was hot out. Many Chinese seemed to admire my outfit, thinking it was the new Western fashion trend.

Nine months! I never want to go through that again. I was still working then, so at least I could keep myself busy without playing sports and get my exercise by hobbling around the block multiple times on crutches. COVID isolation brought about an unpleasant flashback to my Achilles isolation. If it were to happen now . . . I hate to think about it. So I don't.

While recovering from hernia surgery, I find myself pondering the nature of happiness and what constitutes a happy life. Nothing could better illustrate how desperately bored I am than that I'm undertaking a course of thought that risks undermining my lifetime habit of eschewing self-examination. I promise myself that I won't allow my thoughts to cross into self-examination. I'll think about happiness generally, with only the most superficial consideration of my own life. Can I trust myself to keep such a promise given my history of self-sabotage and deception? We'll see.

Unsurprisingly, I don't come up with anything profound. Equally unsurprisingly, the lack of profundity doesn't dissuade me from sharing my thoughts with you.

A friend has an offensive theory he calls *a sunny day in Auschwitz*. He postulates that on a sunny day, when a concentration camp internee found a potato skin on the ground, he was happier than a billionaire entertaining a pair of sex-crazed supermodels on his megayacht might be when his ice machine goes on the fritz or the cocaine falls overboard.[58]

In a similar vein, an oft-cited study of paraplegics and lottery winners found that one year after the paralyzing incident and the megamillion win, both groups had reverted to their pre-event level of happiness.

I had a client, a doorman at an upscale East Side apartment building, who won the lottery and had to hide out under an assumed name to avoid his ex-wives' process servers, greedy relatives, and acquaintances who suddenly claimed to be his best friends. Ultimately, he adjusted to being rich; people are amazingly resilient. He'd never know if people were with him for him or his money. But if he mastered the art of the unexamined life, he wouldn't care as long as they sucked up to him without being too obvious about it.

As alluded to in the introduction, the Four Noble Truths form the basis of Buddhism: (1) life consists of suffering, pain, and misery; (2) this suffering is caused by selfish craving and personal desire; (3) this selfish craving can be overcome; and (4) the way to overcome this misery is through the Eightfold Path. With all due respect to the Awakened One, however, my experience has been precisely the opposite. Having goals and desires and striving to satisfy them have consistently led to my happiness. As a junkyard dog, I thrive on conflict. Similarly, multimillionaires, who have all the money they'd ever have a use for, keep trying to accumulate more. They love the game even more than money—achieving their

---

[58] He also said, "I haven't had sex in so long I forget whose job it is to bring the handcuffs." And that tells you more about him than you need to know. By the way, he's also the one who said supermodel Elle Macpherson was an 8 at best. You might say I need new friends. Maybe someone will read this autobiography and decide to get to know me better. Hey, stop laughing. That wasn't supposed to be a joke.

ends and accumulating more and more moola counts for them as points in the game. Few in their prime of life retreat to a Zen monastery or retire to their own version of Tiberius Caesar's Capri or Jeffrey Epstein's private Caribbean island to indulge in every desired licit or illicit pleasure. They just set more inflated goals and keep striving.

Phew! So far at least, I've successfully navigated between the Scylla of abject boredom and the Charybdis of examining my life, and I've come up with a pretentious literary reference in the bargain.

In any event, when cleared for sports, I return to my happy, busy life, appreciating it more after the surgical interruption. COVID recedes in the rearview mirror, even if, as it says on those mirrors, "Objects in the Rearview Mirror Are Closer Than They Appear."

I asked one of my tennis partners, a former Greek ambassador to the United States and director of the Onassis Foundation if he'd hit with me. Failing to take into consideration his preternatural competitiveness, I explain, "I'm not yet cleared to play games. My doctor tells me not to serve because that could strain my abdominal muscles, and I shouldn't run hard. Rallying, though, would be fine if that's okay with you. If not, we can wait a couple of weeks to play."

"No problem," he replies. "We can hit for twenty minutes, then play a set."

He habitually neglects to wear his hearing aid in the belief that doing so makes him look old, although not being able to hear not only makes him appear older—it also makes talking to him frustrating. Now, though, complying with my request, he puts in his hearing aid; and I reiterate my restrictions and that if he wants to wait another two weeks, we could then play games. He replies that hitting and not playing is fine but then reiterates what he'd said earlier about playing after twenty minutes, this time adding that he's going to kick my ass and administer to me the beating I so richly deserve.

Seeing no point to re-reiterate what I'd said, I came up with a solution: "We'll just hit, but you'll get a point for every ball you hit to me without my having to run for the ball and lose one for each one you miss or hit beyond my reach. I'll lose a point each time I miss, but only if I could've reached your ball without having to run."

That's fine with him. We rally. He chortles and raises a triumphant fist whenever I miss a shot and takes great pleasure in beating me. Okay with me, I enjoy getting back on the court and interacting with a friend.

Still, he wasn't as competitive as the orthopedic surgeon with whom I used to play. After every match, he took the can of balls home and wrote on it the score, date, and name of his opponent. Those mementos filled the entire coat closet in his apartment; and he had near-perfect recall of the details of every match we played, including each of my supposedly bad calls and allegedly lucky shots, although *his* bad calls and lucky shots slipped his mind.

Unlike them, I'm not competitive. I play for the love of the game, which is markedly greater when I whup the fuckers' asses than when I lose, often due to an inexplicable fluke, my opponent's bad calls, or maybe a rigged game.

From time to time, I worry about what will happen when decrepitude hits, and I can no longer play sports or even wipe my own ass. How to navigate the space between to be and not to be, that is a question that I can't force from my mind. My life would be much improved if I were to cease concerning myself with the future as I had in "my salad days when I was green in judgment."[59] After all, the unexamined life has so far turned out pretty well for me, all things—or rather a self-selected number of things—considered. It's proverbially ill-advised to change horses in midstream, and I'm much closer to the fatal far bank than I am to the middle of life's river. Also, the only time I actually rode a horse, my ass hurt for a week. Sorry for the cliché, but I thought this would be a good place for the common touch after having so recently referenced both Shakespeare and the *Odyssey*.

Life is good. I'm happily socializing with friends, playing sports, taking courses, and writing humorous pieces. This turns out to be one of the most pleasant periods of my life. While it lacks the excitement of living with Ann, being with Sally, bringing in a major piece of business, or winning a big case, it also lacks the painful unpleasantness of rejection, abusive bosses, sucking up to unpleasant clients, dealing with a dysfunctional court system, and fighting with partners.

Now busy and healthy, there's no reason to continue writing. You deserve a better ending, perhaps a tearful, but joyful account of my funeral and the multitudinous weeping attendees. But I can't very well write about that without losing credibility. Anyway, as you might have already noticed, we rarely get what we deserve. The evil that men do lives after them. The good is oft interred with their bones. Just came up with that. Pretty good, eh?

Then six months later, everything turns to shit; and bored and in desperation, I again pick up my metaphorical pen.

---

[59] I'm not sure what that means, but this seemed to be a good place to class up this autobiography with a Shakespearean quotation.

XXXVII

Fuck!

May–August 2023

I had an on-and-off pain in my left foot. It started to hurt when I walked more than a few blocks and when I played tennis. However, I could walk and play through the pain, and it generally went away after a while. At my age, either something hurts somewhere, or you're dead. Catering to every ache and pain means never getting out of bed and then being plagued by bedsores. Always in character, Amy suggested I consult a doctor. But most such maladies cure themselves over time, albeit the more time, the older one gets. Anyway, it didn't seem to be getting worse. Also, even if it didn't get better, it wasn't as much of an inconvenience as staying off my foot or wearing a surgical boot would've been, which would have been a doctor's likely recommendation or, God forbid, surgery. I'd already had enough of that.

With Congress closed for Easter break, Adam had two weeks off from his work for the bipartisan Select Committee on the Chinese Communist Party. He, Amy, and I celebrated Passover at Amy's sister's Brooklyn brownstone. It's wonderful to be participating in family holidays again. The next day, we went to Vienna and Rome, our first vacation since COVID. When we travel, we walk, often ten miles a day. Curiously, Amy, who smokes cigarettes and does no exercise, walked our asses off. At least Adam had an excuse for his occasional end-of-day fatigue. In addition to our long walks, he ran five hilly miles every day before we set out, and he still had far more energy at the end of the day than me. Only partly due to my aching foot, which got worse as the trip progressed, I struggled to keep up, lagging behind Amy and Adam while they navigated our route, making me feel abandoned. Just the same, it was good to be on vacation, primarily as I had the opportunity to spend extended time with my son; and he seemed to be enjoying the trip. One day, he'll have his own family—I can only hope—and a demanding job and wouldn't have the time or inclination to travel with us. So we'd better enjoy his presence while we can.

Rome was the more interesting city, perhaps partially because we were in Vienna for only two and a half days and didn't have the opportunity to explore the countryside or take advantage of the city's renown opportunities to listen to classical music and enjoy opera (because *enjoy opera* was an oxymoron for Amy and me). As impressive as the Roman ruins were, they were a bit depressing because they are, well, *ruins*; and their deterioration saddened me. I thought about how overwhelming and spectacular the late Roman Republic and early imperial Rome were with their brightly painted monumental public buildings, large open public fora, and the patricians' grand villas—more impressive than any public space built in the last few hundred years, particularly when one takes into consideration that they were constructed with primitive methods (best not to think about slave labor in this context, particularly as all great minds of the age—Jesus, Socrates, Cicero, etc.—accepted slavery as the normal order of things). To my surprise, however, I was most intrigued by Renaissance Rome. Prejudiced by the Protestant/Enlightenment propaganda served up to me in school, I'd thought of the Renaissance popes as corrupt, degenerate, hypocritical hedonists indifferent to the teachings of Jesus or the welfare of their flocks. On our trip, I realized they were among the most educated and sophisticated of their contemporaries, who financed, encouraged, and facilitated extraordinary advances in art, architecture, and culture. As history is written by the winners (a corollary to today's situation where cable news is presented to placate the losers), I try to be open-minded and ready to put aside my preconceived opinions.

We took a number of inspiring tours, including one of the basement of the Amphitheatrum Flavium (the Colosseum),[60] which had previously been closed to tourists. There, we saw the mechanisms used to flood the arena for mock naval battles and to lift the animals and gladiators onto the field of conflict. My favorite tour, however, was Bernini and Borromini: Battle in Baroque, during which we visited several spectacularly ornate baroque and rococo churches. The Borghese Gallery, with its extraordinary collection of Renaissance art, came in at a close second.

On our last afternoon in Rome, we split up. Amy had a massage, and Adam got more deeply into the Roman ruins than I wanted to. I immediately regretted not going with him since spending time with him was my prime goal and ancient Rome fascinated me. But anyway, I took a long walk through the Villa Borghese, then to a villa several miles away while I listened to podcasts and took the occasional photograph with my phone. Shortly after I reached my destination, my phone died, depriving me of entertainment and, more importantly, Google Maps. Unable even to call a cab, I was relegated

---

[60] Recently, a tourist carved his name and that of his girlfriend in the Colosseum. His excuse: he didn't know it was so old. Experts have charted the excess deaths from COVID. If they did the same for the stupidity-caused deaths related to the general failure of education, the number would be astronomical.

to asking directions from strangers, who felt compelled to try to help even if they had no idea how to get to where I wanted to go and often sent me off in the wrong direction. I had a map, but as it showed only main streets, it was useless. By the time I finally made it back to the hotel, I was exhausted and footsore. It was incomprehensible how the ancient and renaissance Romans managed to get by without cell phones. I seemed to recall that I'd done without them for most of my life, but perhaps my memory was playing tricks on me.

On our return, I resumed my busy, satisfying schedule of tennis, Ping-Pong, improv, academic classes, and socializing and continued to ignore the pain in my foot, which had been aggravated by all the walking on the trip. I told Amy that, when I found an opening in my schedule, I'd make an appointment to see an orthopedist. It's astounding all the things I do for Amy. I hope she appreciates them.

You might wonder why I wasted your time by writing about this particular vacation while having not even mentioned our many previous trips other than a passing reference to the one to China. Even I don't know if I'm stalling or building up the suspense.

In any event, before I had the chance to see a doctor, I ran for a ball that skipped off the line between the singles court and the doubles alley. I heard a pop, felt a sharp pain in my left shin, and fell hard. FUCK! I'd torn my tibialis anterior tendon, the one that connects the foot to the shinbone, making it possible to tilt the foot up. An unusual injury, I'm told, but I'm an unusual guy.

The surgeon postulated that, a couple of months before, I'd torn the tendon slightly; and it might have healed if tended to. But by persisting to ignore the pain, as I had so often done with past aches and pains, I'd exacerbated the injury, finally tearing the tendon completely. If true (and on that, I'm agnostic), deciding to play through the pain, against Amy's advice, was another poorly thought-out decision. At least I'm consistent. Perhaps my thoughtlessness and lack of self-examination are foolish consistencies of the type that one of the great minds of the nineteenth century characterized as the "hobgoblin of little minds." Luckily, I don't believe in hobgoblins and have never contemplated the size of my mind relative to that of others.

I had surgery a few days later, and the surgeon sentenced me to eight weeks in a boot cast. During the first six weeks, he prohibited me from putting *any* weight on my left foot—the sort of cruel and unusual punishment the Founding Fathers had in mind when they promulgated the Eighth Amendment. Tennis and even Ping-Pong verboten for *at least* six months.

I left the hospital with a walker, a difficult and awkward way to get around, as I wasn't permitted to walk behind it but only to hop on my right leg. I had crutches. But Amy, in her usual abundance of caution, didn't want me to use them outside. If I fell or even took an awkward slip, the force could rip out the pin that bound the repaired tendon to a fragile bone in my foot. Then I'd be even worse off than before my operation and likely never fully recover. I took her advice, in part because she was taking care of me—I couldn't even prepare my own meals. More importantly, though, as you've already seen, she had the irritating habit of generally being right or at least sensible. I also had a scooter contraption on which I could rest my left leg while using the right for locomotion but putting pressure on my left knee hurt. As a result of my knee replacement, my left knee doesn't bend as far as it should. According to my knee surgeon, that resulted from not having pursued my physical therapy assiduously enough, failing to ignore the pain, and pushing for maximum pain instead of stopping when my therapist told me to. The central tenet of the surgeons' Hypocritical oath is "First, never admit that you did harm." Anything that goes wrong in surgery is always their patients' fault even though they were unconscious at the time of the operation.

With nothing better to do, I return to writing this damn autobiography.

I spend a month and a half sitting in a rocking chair, occasionally taking my knee walker to the park across the street from my building and sitting on a bench. There, I watch the old people feeding bread bits to pigeons, nodding off with spittle leaking from their mouths, or babbling incoherently to their caregivers, who ignore them while surfing the web or chatting on their phones. My first reaction is I never want to be like them. My second is the realization that I already am, although perhaps I'll recover.

I'm in a constant state of panic. Will I slip with the crutches[61] on the way to the bathroom? Will I, in the process of getting up or down from my rocking chair, slip or accidentally put weight on my left leg, catastrophically reinjuring the tendon? Like a nightmarish LSD flashback, my mind recapitulates the depression and diminished capacity for pleasure that resulted from the COVID lockdown and my isolation when suffering from that virus. This time, though, it's even worse. During the lockdown, everyone suffered alike. The total isolation when I had the disease was *only* for ten days, and I had no fear of further debilitating injury, and even then I slipped into depression.

I again fall into depression, and the fact that I so easily succumb to despondency only adds to my sadness. Fear of entering a period of extreme sadness has haunted me most of my adult life.

---

[61] I gave up hopping on one leg behind the walker, and the spaces in our apartment don't accommodate the knee walker.

Regretfully, I'm not bipolar since I don't have ecstatic manic episodes. Also, my depressions have never been so deep that I can't get out of bed. Just the same, I've suffered many periods of profound sadness often accompanied by feelings of abject loneliness. Is such loneliness common? From what I've read, it's becoming more so. It's distressing that I can't even consider myself to be unique, although I can take pride in being ahead of the curve. Being part of a great mass of people plagued by occasional feelings of abject loneliness doesn't make me feel less lonely. I often feel like asking Amy to hug me but having to ask undermines the effort.

Once a day, weather permitting and, like on 9/11, it's almost perfect tennis weather, I sit with friends on a park bench, like the old man I am, my knee scooter beside me. Or I go for short knee scooter trips to the park with Amy. My life encompasses a park bench, a rocking chair in our living room, and Adam's bedroom. Amy has again exiled me to Adam's room because, having to sleep wearing the filthy surgical boot, I not only foul the sheets but also make a mess of the sheets and quilt when I stir. The boot makes sleeping difficult—thank God for Ambien combined with marijuana gummies. Rather than get up to go to the bathroom at night, risking reinjury (particularly if stoned), I again have to pee in a bottle. Also, due to the boot, I go eight weeks without a shower. Washing myself down with a washcloth is a poor substitute; and I never get used to the stench from my unwashed foot in the boot, which never comes off, or the itch from the layer upon layer of skin that has rotted away.

I feel guilty about the burden my incapacity puts on Amy, particularly as she's being so wonderful in caring for me. She has to cancel her Mother's Day trip to visit Adam in Washington, to which she's been looking forward, having not seen him since our trip to

Europe. Also, we can't open the Fire Island house on Memorial Day, as we'd done every year for the past two and a half decades. She leaves me alone for only a couple of hours a day when she goes out for a short walk, does errands, or has lunch with a friend. Otherwise, she's there for me.

Counterintuitively, my injury turns out to be good for our marriage as it draws us closer together. I imagine that, as a result of tending to me, she feels greater affection for me as I had for the cats when I was caring for them during ultimately fatal maladies. It's unsettling, though, how much I like being taken care of. Perhaps it temporarily fills the hole left by being insufficiently loved as a child.

At my five-week appointment with my surgeon, he drops a bomb on me. Yes, I'll be out of the boot three weeks hence. But contrary to what he earlier implied, or which I'd convinced myself I'd heard, he won't clear me for an indeterminate amount of months even for low-impact activities, such as swimming, kayaking, bicycle riding, and walking on a beach. Having been counting the days, hours, and minutes until I could be somewhat active, I, to my shame and embarrassment, broke down in tears. I'm shocked by my mental fragility.

So much for my summer. How many active summers do I have left? Seven at most? Very few people play singles more than a year or two into their eighties. So I'll be out of commission for a significant percentage of the time I have left to be physically able to play tennis.

Maybe for other people who are rarely active and spend most of their days watching TV, playing video games, searching the web, reading, or watching porn, eight weeks of confinement, followed by untold months of highly restricted activity would be a tolerable inconvenience. But for me, it's a disaster.

I've lost confidence in my surgeon. As I know from practicing law, the easiest and safest way for a professional to cover his ass is to prohibit his client from doing anything that brings with it even the smallest scintilla of risk. I don't understand how swimming could reinjure my tendon, and I fear neither does he. It would put less strain on the foot than PT or walking, and the gentle resistance of moving through water would likely help my recovery.

Just the same, I'm not about to take the risk of reinjury and having to go through this hell again only for longer with a positive outcome being less likely. I have to learn to take pleasure from the little things in life and not to need the constant flow of frenzied activity that had, until now, been the key to my happiness. Also, it would be healthy to devise less neurotic ways to fill the hole left by being insufficiently loved as a child. While I'm at it, I should learn to cast all three unforgivable curses outlined in the Harry Potter books: bring peace to the Middle East, and figure out how to live forever— not necessarily in that order.

In an effort to make my confinement tolerable and assert a modicum of control over my situation, I've created a routine, designed in part to ward off dementia in accordance with the frequent articles on staving off Alzheimer's, even though I have no confidence that stimulating my mind will have any positive effect. Each morning, I read the *New York Times* and *Washington Post* and do the mini crossword puzzles in those newspapers and Wordle, Worldle, and Connections. On Mondays and Tuesdays, I do the regular *Times* crosswords (embarrassingly, the rest of the week's puzzles are too tough for me). When I get to the obituaries in the *Times*, all I see is how much older, or *younger*, the deceased were than me. I console myself with the observation that obituaries don't report on the many people who are still alive.

I talk to friends on the phone for at least forty-five minutes a day and watch as much TV as I can stand, which is rarely more than twenty minutes a sitting while I eat. I read until I get sick of doing so, maybe an hour a day. Also, I do some legal work. Once I'm out of the surgical boot, I begin going to the gym. Not great fun, but it's something to do, and I like to listen to podcasts or books on tape while I'm exercising and walking, although I don't have the patience to listen while just sitting. Time creeps by like a crippled snail on Valium. Each day feels like a week, making my eight-week confine-ment feel like fifty-six weeks. The six months—or more likely nine months or even a year, given my surgeon's propensity to move the therapeutic goalposts—without tennis or Ping-Pong feels like an eternity. Tomorrow and tomorrow and tomorrow creeps in this pet-ty pace from day to day, to the last syllable of recorded time. Oh, you've heard that before. Well, maybe the author stole it from me.

My one sustaining passion is writing this autobiography, which I'd abandoned with the loosening of COVID restrictions, took up again when recovering from my hernia, and again now that I'm disabled. When I craft a clever turn of phrase or an amus-ing story, I enjoy writing far more than reading, watching TV, or even sitting on my rocking chair, wallowing in self-pity about my torn tendon. When I get into writing, time passes quickly; and on occasion, I allow myself to fantasize about catching the inter-est of a publisher or even persuading someone to make it into a major motion picture, with me playing the lead and in charge of casting sexy starlets to play the parts of Sally, Ann, or Elizabeth. Sometimes I feel that what I'm writing is brilliant—genius even.

But when I read that stuff the next day, I realize it's puerile crap. Mostly, though, I'm immune to self-delusion; and my dreams shrink to self-publishing and persuading a handful of friends to buy it and then claim, with a straight face, to have enjoyed it.

When the words don't flow, though, writing feels like an unpleasant job, one for which I'm not getting paid; and each sentence I write comes out even clunkier than the previous one. George Fowler, whoever the hell he was, said, "Writing is easy. You only need to stare at a blank piece of paper until drops of blood form on your forehead." No matter, writing gets me through these hard, lonely times. Indeed, I worry about what I'll do when I complete the book.

It occurs to me that maybe my shtick about being insufficiently loved as a child is a self-serving justification for feelings of inadequacy and generally being an asshole. I'm increasingly struck by how difficult it is to really know anything. That's one of the problems of the examined life, collateral damage that accompanies writing this autobiography. Unfortunately, writing is about the only activity that alleviates my boredom. Examining my life leads to a problem analogous to Heisenberg's uncertainty principle—the deeper I examine my life, the less I know with any degree of certainty. It's also like one of the central principles of Daoism—those who know do not speak; those who speak do not know. And I've done a shitload of speaking or at least writing, which in this case is the functional equivalent.

Just the same, keeping you people amused has become something of a strain; and I fear that lately, I've been letting you down. Maybe you think this chapter has so far been boring but be thankful that you haven't had to actually live through it.

For my comic sketch writing class course, I'm required to write a sketch each week. When I get an assignment, my first reaction is to panic. Sure, I'll be unable to come up with anything. After a day of agonizing, an idea comes to me, like an epiphany from the Almighty; and I write my first draft in an hour of near ecstasy. Even though this is a long-established pattern, each time I remind myself that I've always come up with something to write, often something pretty good, that doesn't allay the initial panic.

My friends are being terrific. Twice a week, one of them comes to the Upper West Side to sit with me in the park, often bringing lunch or dinner for which they refuse to let me reimburse them. I haven't played squash in over three decades. But two friends from my squash days, who've moved out of New York, call every couple of weeks to chat and see how I'm doing, as do two former tennis friends who moved to Florida more than a decade ago and three law school friends who live out of town.

Their concern and, more than that, their company, whether in person or on the phone, help make my long convalescence tolerable. I hope I'm sufficiently expressing my appreciation for them. Their help confirms for me the importance of visiting the infirm. If they ever have a problem, I'll be there for them. Realizing that I have a number of good friends is an inspiring revelation. We enjoyed one another's company for years, but I never needed their help and didn't know if they'd be there for me if I did.

I've repeatedly groused in these pages about having lost contact with numerous buddies due to my having retired into COVID lockdown, but it's turned out that I've also retained many close friends. Earlier in this autobiography, I referenced happiness studies that emphasized the importance of keeping up with friendships and generally maintaining relationships. My tendon convalescence experience drove that home to me. I'm proud that I've made and kept up with so many friends. I must have been a decent friend to them over the years.

Come late June, when I'm finally able to take care of myself, although still confined to the surgical boot, Amy moves out to Fire Island for the remainder of the summer. I can't go with her while I'm still confined to the boot, if only because the boot would scuff our white floors. Fourth of July week, Adam comes out to Fire Island. I can't join him until the end of the week when I finally get the boot off. He and I overlap for part of one day. When will there be another chance to spend a week with Adam? Surely, there will be few such opportunities. Sad.

Once out of the boot, I stay in Manhattan on weekdays to do physical therapy and take courses in improv and comic sketch writing. I miss Amy, maybe even as much as I miss playing sports. Although now able to join Amy on Fire Island on weekends, all I'm permitted to do is walk the paved paths and read in the shade; with the prospect of being able to resume activity in a few months, it would be a stone drag to come down with serious skin cancer. Watching everyone else playing tennis, swimming, kayaking, swimming in the bay, hanging out at the beach, and frolicking in the surf doesn't raise my spirits.

I've texted my sister several times, telling her about my surgical confinement. But she doesn't have time for me, never calling and rarely texting to see how I'm doing. However, in Fire Island, I enjoy the company of Amy's sister's family, including my grandnieces and grandnephew and my nephews, who, unlike my niece and nephew by blood, always get in touch when they're in town.

While Amy is in Fire Island, I need an endoscopy, and someone has to pick me up and take me home. I don't want to burden Amy with coming into the city for that task, given all the inconvenience my invalidism has already imposed on her. So Brewie picks me up, takes me home, and acts like it's a pleasure to do so.

My surgeon finally clears me to play Ping-Pong if I wear the cumbersome surgical boot. So I play with a friend in Fire Island and then walk in his pool (without the boot). It's one of the best events in my life—not quite up to the day Adam was born or my second wedding, but comparable to my first night with Ann and storming the Pentagon with Sally. Tennis is still two months away, but at last, I'm making progress.

I have no doubt that you're fed up with my constant bitching, particularly as, by any objective standard, I've had it pretty good. Hard to have much sympathy for an old white man, unless you're the old white man in question.

Particularly with the world in such a god-awful mess. The handful of far-right lunatics, who inexplicably control Congress, whine about the deficit but seek to decrease taxes on the rich and suggest no spending cuts other than defunding the IRS. Like petulant children indifferent to consequences and needing to be the center of attention, they court publicity by shutting down the government. In the face of the existential disaster of an autocratic kakistocracy,[62] the Democrats are fielding an inarticulate, unpopular octogenarian, widely perceived to be senile, and his universally disliked vice president—thereby assuring that many of their traditional constituencies—young people, Black men, Latinos, Muslims, and

---

[62] Rule of the worst, from Greek

tens of millions of alienated citizens—won't vote and guaranteeing a second Trump presidency, but for a miracle[63]. Whistling past the abattoir, Dems, ensconced in their bubble, utter delusional drivel like "He won last time" and "All my friends will vote for him." Trump intends to hand Ukraine to Putin, dismantle NATO, and harness the full power of the federal government to seek *retribution* against his enemies, immigrants and minorities. Maybe there'll be a euphemism for *concentration camps*, but why bother? He'll ignore, and even accelerate, climate change. More than 20 million people each year are already forced to leave their homes as a result of extreme weather events, and that number will accelerate logarithmically.

Oops, another angry rant slipped out. Well, sympathetic or not, I cherish my God-given right to bitch. After all, pursuant to the Declaration of Independence, I'm "endowed by [my] Creator with certain unalienable Rights, that among these are Life, Liberty and the pursuit of Happiness." It's beyond cavil that the pursuit of happiness encompasses the right to bitch, particularly if one is Jewish.

Something just occurred to me: perhaps I should stop watching cable news and confine my obsessions to things I can control.

My injury hasn't been an unalloyed negative. In addition to improving my relationship with Amy, it's made me appreciate my friends more and vow to be a better friend to them. Although, as my dad would say, the race hasn't yet been run, it turns out that, Socrates notwithstanding, *both* the examined and unexamined lives are worth living. Life may be suffering, as the Buddha said. But sometimes that suffering is quite pleasurable, such as when I was mooning over Sally and my broken heart. One step forward for a man, a nonevent for mankind.

---

[63] Most people I know disagree. I hope they're right

Once I return to regular activity, I appreciate all those activities more than I had. Still, my years of being able to play sports are limited at best, so I'd better learn to enjoy more passive activities. Perhaps my confinement was good practice for the future, and maybe it even taught me to find pleasure in what I'm capable of doing rather than resent not being able to do those things that gave me pleasure when I was younger.

At the last hearing of the bipartisan Select Committee on the Chinese Communist Party, its chairman, Mike Gallagher, used his opportunity to sum up the proceedings to instead extravagantly praise Adam's work for the committee as well as his character and legal ability. It was so unexpected and moving that it brought tears to my eyes, and it's part of the Congressional Record.

Something so bizarre and unanticipated happened that I've waited a week to see if it was real before writing about it. I'm happy, actually happy. I'm still not playing tennis yet, but I've been busy and somewhat productive. Each night, I examine—*examine?*—well, look back on my day. And like God after creating the universe, I see that it was good.

A weird and revolutionary idea comes to me out of nowhere: *maybe I should discard the shit-colored glasses, stop whining about my first-world problems, be thankful for all the good things I have, and just enjoy myself.* As I'm a risk-taker addicted to foolish, self-defeating frolics, I may try that and see how it works out. Frighteningly, my life seems to be turning against my will into an examined one. It's fine for now—but so are meth, cocaine, and heroin at first. At my age, navigating such a slippery slope can be dangerous. I may fall and be unable to get up.

I've now caught up with the present time. It would be appropriate to end here with a wise, eminently quotable maxim or at least a phrase so clever that my readers write it down and put it in their wallets like my dad's joke list. But shockingly, none come to me. Endings are hard.

So, copping out as usual, I'm tacking on a dark fantasy about Adam in the future that contains as much of a glimmer of hope as I can imagine given the color of my glasses, which I still wear from time to time, and the perilous political situation and unhappy state of the world.

The high school friend who'd referred to me my largest client has a standard toast: "We're still here and not publicly disgraced."

Amen. Could be a lot worse and surely will be.

XXXVIII

The Bad Grandpa

2050

It's weird being seventy-five and probably would be even if these were more normal times. It's got me thinking, worrying about what life will be like when my son, Adam, reaches my age. I can only hope he does, but it's hard to be optimistic about what he'll find.

Adam—a fit man in his early seventies, wearing jeans, a faded Philadelphia Eagles T-shirt, and a tattered backpack—waits at the entrance to an underground bunker. A metal door slides open with a screech. Adam's son, Burke, stands on the inside, arms akimbo. Adam's grandchildren, Confucius (known as Connie) and Lao-Tze (known as Leo), jump to their feet, delighted to see him.

"WTF, Dad?" Burke looks indistinct as he's standing behind the semitransparent decontamination chamber.

"As you may recall, from three hours ago, you mentally messaged me to sit for the kids because you and Ayn have to be in your work pods all day."

"I didn't say dress like a throwback to last century. Where's your PPE?"

"We've had this conversation, but only a hundred times," Adam says. "Having lived through COVID-19, 27, and 31, I'm immune."

"With Donald IV renegotiating the Chinese loans, they're watching everyone in an effort to demonstrate to the CCP that we're as vigilant in stamping out errors as they are. They'll downgrade your social credit rating to nonpersonhood. You're already on the cusp."

"I'm too old to care. Maybe they'll realize I'm a lost cause— grandfathered in." Adam chuckles. He's always enjoyed his own attempts at humor.

The door to the cylindrical decontamination chamber slides open. Adam steps in. It fills with mist. When it clears, a door on the far side slides open. Adam descends into the underground residence.

"Sorry about the hostile undertone. Stressful times these," Burke says. "Good to see you. Virtual hug." He extends his arms.

Adam does the same. Does Burke remember actual hugs, handshakes, kisses? Those were the days. Or were they? Adam's not sure.

"I'm delighted to help, but why can't the robot watch the kids?"

"It's on the fritz," Burke says, face turning red.

"Mommy said something bad about the beloved Chinese leaders, so they decommissioned the robot." Connie giggles, knowing that with Adam here, she'll get away with telling on her mother.

"Good break for me." Adam smiles. Maybe he'll sneak a hug with the kids after his son enters his work pod.

"Dad, help yourself to the fooderizer. But please, no roughhousing with the kids." Turning toward his children, Burke drops his voice. "You don't have to do everything your grandfather tells you to."

"Good point. Look how my son turned out as a result of my parenting."

Burke leaves. Adam tosses a present to Connie. She makes a clumsy effort to catch it. It rolls along the floor, then stops. Leo prods at it.

"How does it turn on?"

"It's a football," Adam says. "It's always on."

"What do we do with it?" Connie asks.

"Throw it, catch it, kick it, run with it." Adam continues in a conspiratorial whisper. "Let's go outside. I'll show you."

"Outside?" Leo asks, his voice a modulated shriek. "Mommy would lose her shit . . . and her social credit rating. Anyway, we can't run, throw, or catch in our outside PPEs."

"Why would we want to throw it?" Connie screws up her face. "You once . . . told us about a big war between eagles, cowboys, redskins, and giants. It involved a football."

"Tell us a story about when there were animals," Leo says.

"There are lots of animals now," Connie says. "Cockroaches, rats."

"I'm talking about big ones—pigs, cows, elephants," Leo says.

"I used to eat bacon, steak, and prosciutto," Adam says as much to himself as to them.

They laugh, although their confused facial expressions communicate that they have no idea what he's talking about.

"Were you alive when Christ returned and Donald I told him he prefers sons of God who weren't crucified?" Connie asks.

"Daddy told us you lived in Manhattan before everyone realized it was part of China and President Donald Jr. gave it back to them," Leo says.

Adam tosses the football to Leo, who, to his surprised delight, catches it.

"Let me try," Connie says.

Adam throws it to her. She catches it, then tosses it to her brother. The three of them lateral the ball back and forth, running around the room and laughing until the kids are exhausted.

"That was fun!" Leo exclaims through heaving breaths. "Did you have fun before you went crazy from the virus and the disinfectant the Trumpers made you drink?"

"No, I was a lawyer."

"Mommy says you're still a liar," Connie says, her troublemaker mode returning.

"If I said that wasn't true, would you believe me?"

"I would," Leo says, but then his momentary bravado fades. "If the Chinese let me."

Made in United States
North Haven, CT
30 September 2024

58115645R00162